A BRIEF LIFE OF CHRIST

FULTON J. SHEEN

A Brief Life of Christ

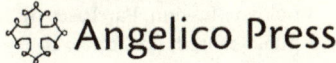
Angelico Press

Angelico Press reprint edition, 2011
This Angelico edition is a slightly altered
republication of the work originally published by
the Maco Magazine Corporation, New York, NY, in 1954

No part of this book may be reproduced or transmitted,
in any form or by any means, without permission

For information, address:
Angelico Press, P.O. Box 151011
San Rafael, CA 94915
angelicopress.com

978-1-887593-94-6
978-1-621385-65-3

Cover Design: Cristy Deming
Image Credit: James Tissot (French, 1836–1902).
The Baptism of Jesus (Baptême de Jésus), 1886–1894.
Opaque watercolor over graphite on gray wove paper,
Image: 8½ x 5½ in. (21.6 x 14 cm).
Brooklyn Museum, Purchased by
public subscription, 00.159.49

CONTENTS

Early Life of Christ	1
Temptations	18
The Beatitudes	36
Public Life and Passion	51
Death and Resurrection	68

Dedicated to

the Mother of Christ

who stood beneath the Cross

and shared Compassion with Passion

and through His Mandate became the Mother of Men

Early Life of Christ

HISTORY is full of men who said that they came from God, or that they were gods, or that they bore a message from God. Buddha, Mohammed, Confucius, Christ, Socrates, Lao-Tze and thousands of others—each has a right to be heard for his claims. There must be tests to decide whether the claims to divinity are justified. These tests, available to all men, all civilizations and all ages, are two-fold: *reason* and *history*. *Reason*, because everyone has it, even those without faith; *history*, because everyone lives in it, and should know something about it.

Our reason tells us that if any of the claimants came from God, the least that God could do to support his claim would be to preannounce his coming. Automobile manufacturers tell us when to expect a new model. If God is sending anyone from Himself with the most important message for all men, He owes it to us to let us know *when* the Messenger is coming, *where* He will be born, *where* He will live, the *doctrine* He will teach, the *enemies* He will make, the *program* He will adopt for the future, and the manner of His *death*. By His conformity with these announcements, we could judge Him.

Reason further tells us that if God does not do this, then there is nothing to prevent any fool from appearing in history and saying: "I am from God," or "An angel appeared to me in the desert and gave me this message." In such a case there is no objective, historical test for such a messenger. We have just his word for it, and he could be suffering a delusion.

If a visitor came from a foreign country to Washington, and said he was a diplomat, we would ask to see his passport and his credentials. His papers would have to antedate his coming. If we ask for such proofs of identity from diplomats, we certainly ought to do so in the all-important subject of religion, asking: "What record is there before you were born that you were coming?"

With this test in mind, line up the claimants. Include anyone you please for, at the moment, Christ is no greater than any of them. We now address them: "Socrates, did anyone know you were coming?" "Gotama, did anyone ever preannounce you and your message, and predict that one day you would sit under the Buddha tree?" "Mohammed, was the place of your birth recorded, and given to men centuries before, so that when you did come, men would know you were a messenger from God?" "Christ, did anyone know of Your coming, the circumstances of Your life, where You would live?"

All are silent—but one. There were no predictions about Buddha, Mohammed, or anyone else—except Christ. Others just came and said: "Here I am, believe me." They were, therefore, men among men, and not the Divine in the human, which is the kind of leader we want for these hard times. Christ, alone, steps out of the line and answers: "My coming was foretold, even to the smallest detail."

Early Life of Christ

He tells us to search the writings of the Jewish people and the correlated history of the Babylonians, Persians, Greeks and Romans, and for the moment, to regard their writings merely as historical documents, not as inspired writings. The Person of Christ in passing this test of reason and history speaks:

> About two thousand years before I was born, there appeared a man, Abraham, as the head of people in whom 'all the nations of the earth would be blessed.' About two thousand years before I was born, it was foretold that He Who would be born among the people of Abraham, would be also the 'expected of the nations', that is, of the Gentiles as well as the Jews. About seven hundred years before I was born, it was foretold that I would be born in Bethlehem, and that even though born in time, I already had an eternal birth.
>
> Not only was My birthplace foretold, but about seven hundred years before, it was foretold that I would be born of a Virgin! 'A Virgin shall conceive and bring forth a son, and His name shall be called Emmanuel.' About seven hundred years before I was born, it was foretold that the Kings of the East would bring gold and frankincense and myrrh, that I would sojourn to Egypt, and that I would live in Nazareth. About six hundred years before I was born, it was foretold that I would come within a set period after Cyrus gave out the order for

A BRIEF LIFE OF CHRIST

rebuilding the walls of Jerusalem. About five hundred years before I was born, it was foretold that My name would be Jesus or Saviour.

Even the details of My character were preannounced, namely, that I would be kind, console the afflicted, be rejected by My own people. The details of My death were foretold: Centuries before, it was prophesied that there would be wounds in My hands and feet, that My enemies would shake dice for My garments, and yet in putting Me to death, they would not break a bone of My body. A thousand years before, it was foretold that at My death I would be given vinegar and gall in My thirst.

Six centuries before My birth, it was preannounced that I would ascend into heaven. So many prophecies were made concerning Me that at the time of My coming, the ancient synagogues collected 456 distinct prophecies. And it was not only the people of Israel who expected Me, but all the other peoples of the world.

We turn now to pagan testimony. Tacitus, speaking for the ancient Romans, says: "People were generally persuaded in the faith of the ancient prophecies, that the East was to prevail, and that from Judea was to come the master and ruler of the world."

Suetonius, in his life of Vespasian, recounting the Roman tradition also said: "It was an old and constant belief throughout the East, that by indubitably certain

Early Life of Christ

prophecies, the Jews were to attain the highest power." China had the same expectation but, because it was on the other side of the world, believed that the great Wise Man would be born in the West. The Annals of the Celestial Empire state: "In the 24th year of Tchao-Wang of the dynasty of the Chou, on the 8th day of the 4th moon, a light appeared in the southwest which illumined the king's palace. The monarch, struck by its splendor, interrogated the sages. They showed him books in which this prodigy signified the appearance of the great Saint of the West whose religion was to be introduced into their country."

The Greeks expected Him, for Aeschylus in his Prometheus, six centuries before His coming, wrote: "Look not for any end moreover to this curse until God appears, to accept upon His Head the pangs of thy own sins vicarious."

How did the Magi of the East know of His coming, if it was not from the many prophesies circulated through the world by the Jews and probably through the prophecy made to the Persians by Daniel more than 500 years before His Birth?

Cicero, after recounting the ancient oracles and Sibyls about a "King whom we must recognize to be saved", asked in expectation: "What man and of what period of time do these predictions point?" The Fourth Eclogue of Virgil recounted the same ancient tradition and spoke of a "chaste woman, smiling on her infant boy, with whom the Iron Age would pass away."

Suetonius quotes a contemporary author to the effect that the Romans were so fearful about a King who would rule the world, that they ordered all children born that year to be killed—an order that was not fulfilled, except by Herod.

Not only were the Jews expecting the birth of a Great King, a Wise Man and a Saviour, but Plato also spoke of the Logos; Socrates, of the Universal Wise Man "yet to come"; Confucius, of "the Saint"; the Sibyls, of a "Universal King"; the Greek Dramatist, of a Saviour and Redeemer to unloose the "primal eldest curse".

What separates Christ from all men is first, He was expected. Even the Gentiles had a longing for some deliverer or redeemer. This fact alone differentiates Him from all other religious leaders.

The second fact is that once He appeared, He hit history with such an impact that He split it in two, dividing all history into the period previous to His coming, and the period after His coming. Buddha did not do this, nor did any of the Indian philosophers. Even those who deny God must date their attacks upon Him as done in A.D. (*anno Domini*)—so many years after His coming.

The third fact which separates Him from all others is this: *Every other person who came into this world, came into it to live. He came into it to die.* Death was a stumbling block to Socrates—it interrupted his teaching. But to Christ, death was the goal of His life, the gold that He was seeking. Few of His words or actions are intelligible, unless we keep in mind His Cross. He presented Himself as a Saviour, rather than a Teacher. It meant nothing to teach men to be good, unless He gave them the *power* to be good, after rescuing them from the

Early Life of Christ

frustration of guilt. John gives His Eternal pre-history; Matthew His temporal pre-history in his genealogy. What is significant about it is how much his ancestry is tied up with sinners and with foreigners! There are four women mentioned: Thamar, a harlot; Rahab, another; Ruth, the Moabitess, and Bathsheba. Three of them are tainted as regards womanly purity, and one, though morally good, had alien blood in her veins. These "blots on the escutcheon" of His human lineage, suggest a pity for the sinful and for the strangers of the covenant. Both such charges would later on be hurled against Him, namely "He is a friend of sinners"; "He is a Samaritan". But the shadow of a stained past beckons to the future love of the stained. Born of a woman, He was a man and could be one with mankind; born of a Virgin, overshadowed by the Spirit and "full of grace", He would be outside that current of sin which infected all humanity.

A fourth fact about Christ is that, unlike other world teachers, He does not fit into the category of a *good man*. Good men do not lie. But if Christ is not all that He said He was, namely, the Son of the Living God, the Word of God in the flesh, then He is *not* "just a good man"—He is a knave, a liar, a charlatan and the greatest deceiver Who ever lived. If He is not what He said He was, the Christ, the Son of God, He is the anti-Christ! But he is not just a good man.

He would have us either worship Him or despise Him—despise Him as a mere man, or worship Him as true God and true Man. That is the alternative He presents.

A BRIEF LIFE OF CHRIST

If He is what He claimed to be, a Saviour, a Redeemer, then we have a virile Christ for these days; someone Who will step into the breach of death and sin and gloom and despair, a Leader to Whom we can make total sacrifice and Whom we can love even unto death. We need a Christ today whose voice will be like the voice of the raging sea, and Who will not allow us to pick and choose among His words, discarding what we do not like, and accepting what pleases our fancy. We need a Christ Who will restore moral indignation, and will make us hate evil with a passionate intensity and love goodness to a point where we will drink death like water.

Even His Birth was a forecast of His Death which was the primary purpose of His coming to this earth. Caesar Augustus, the master bookkeeper of the world, sat in his palace by the Tiber. Before him was stretched a map labelled *Orbis Terrarum, Imperium Romanum*. He was about to issue an order for a census of the world, for then all nations were subject to him. There was only one capital in the world: Rome; only one official language: Latin; only one ruler: Caesar. To every outpost, satrap and governor, the order went out that everyone was to be enrolled in his own city. In the fringe of the empire in a little village of Nazareth, soldiers tacked upon walls the order for every citizen to register in the town of his family's origin.

Joseph, the builder, descendent of the great King David, was obliged to register in the city of David—

Early Life of Christ

Bethlehem. In accordance with that edict, Mary and Joseph set out from the village of Nazareth for the village of Bethlehem, which lay about five miles on the other side of Jerusalem. Five hundred years before the prophet Micheas had prophesied concerning that little village: "Thou Bethlehem are the least of the cities of Judea and out of thee will He come forth Who is to be a ruler in Israel."

Joseph was full of expectancy as he entered the city of his family. He was confident that he would have no difficulty in finding lodgings for Mary, particularly since she was with child. From house to house, Joseph went only to find each one crowded. He sought in vain for a place where might be born the One to Whom heaven and earth belonged. Could it be that the Creator would not be at home in creation?

Up a steep hill he climbed to a faint light swinging on a rope across the doorway which signified the village inn. There he knocked, above all places else, most hopefully. There was room in that inn for the soldiers of Rome who bore on their coats Rome's screaming eagles; there was room for the daughters of the rich merchants of the East; there was room for those clothed in soft garments, who lived in the houses of the king; there was room for those who had a tip to give the inn keeper. But there was no room for Him Who came to be the Inn of every homeless heart in the world. When finally, the scrolls of history will have recorded the last words in the annals of time, the saddest line of all will be:

"There was no room in the inn."

A BRIEF LIFE OF CHRIST

Out to the hillside, to a stable cave, where shepherds drove their flocks in storms, Joseph and Mary went for shelter. There, in a place of peace and tranquility, in the utter abandonment and cold of a windswept cave; there, under the floor of the world, Mary, as a flesh and blood ciborium, lifted up to the gaze of all, the Host of the world. "Behold the Lamb of God Who taketh away the sins of the world." He Who was born without a mother in heaven, was born without a father on earth.

Of every other child born into the world, friends might say that it resembles its mother. This was the first instance in time that any one could say that the Mother resembled the Child. Here was the beautiful paradox of the Child Who made His Mother; therefore, the Mother was only a child. It was also the first time in the history of this earth of ours that anyone could ever think of heaven being anywhere else than "way up there", but Mary now looked down to Heaven.

In the filthiest place in the world, a stable, purity was born. He Who was to be devoured by men acting as beasts, was born amongst beasts. He Who called Himself the "living Bread descended from Heaven" was born in Bethlehem, "the house of bread", and laid in a manger, the place of food. Centuries before, the Jews had worshipped the golden calf and the Greeks had worshipped the ass. Men bowed down before them as before God. The ox and the ass now made their reparation and retribution by bowing down themselves before their God.

There was no room in the inn, but there was room in

Early Life of Christ

the stable. The inn is the gathering place of public opinion, the focal point of the world's moods, the rendezvous of the worldly, the rallying place of the popular. But the stable is a place of outcasts, the ignored, the forgotten, the almost impossible things. If there was any place in all the earth where the world would have expected the Son of God to be born, it would have been in an inn. The stable would be the last place in the world we would have looked for Him. *Divinity is always where we least expect to find it.*

No worldly mind would ever have suspected that He Who could make the sun warm the earth would one day have need of an ox and an ass to warm Him with their breath; that He Who, in the language of Scriptures, could stop the turning about of the Arcturus, would be subject to an imperial edict of a census; that He Who clothed the fields with grass would Himself be naked; that He from Whose finger tips tumbled planets and worlds would one day have tiny hands that were not long enough to touch the huge heads of the cattle; that feet which trod the everlasting hills would one day be too weak to walk; that the Eternal Word would be dumb; that Omnipotence would be wrapped in swaddling clothes; that Salvation would lie in a manger; that the mirth of Heaven would weep; that the bird that built the nest would be hatched therein—no one would ever have suspected that God coming to this earth would ever be so helpless. But that is just precisely why they are apt to miss Him—*Divinity is always where we least expect to find it.*

If the artist is at home in his studio, because the

paintings are the creation of his own mind; if the sculptor is at home amongst his statues, for they were begotten of his brain; if a husbandman is at home among his vines, for he planted them; if the father is at home in his family, because they are his own, then surely, argues the world, He Who made the world should be at home in it; He should come into it as an artist into his studio, and as a Father into his home; but for the Creator to come amongst His creatures and be ignored, for God to come among His own and not to be received by His own, for God to be homeless at home, that to the world can only mean one thing—that that Babe could not be God. But that is just why it missed Him. *Divinity is always where we least expect to find it.*

The Son-of-God-made-man was forced to enter His own world through a back door. Exiled from the earth, He was born under the earth as the First Cave Man of Christian history. There He shook the earth to its very foundations. Being born in a cave, all who entered had to stoop. To stoop is the mark of humility. The proud refused to stoop, and missed Divinity. Those, however, who bent their ego and entered, found they were not in a cave at all, but in a new universe where sat a Babe on His Mother's lap, with the world poised on His fingers.

The manger and the cross thus stand at the two extremities of the Saviour's life: He accepted the manger because there was no room in the inn; He accepted the Cross, because men said: "We will not have this man for our king." Disowned in entrance, rejected in exit. He was laid in a stranger's stable at the beginning, and a stranger's grave at the end. An ox and an ass surrounded His crib at Bethlehem; two thieves would surround His Cross on Calvary. He was wrapped in swaddling bands in His birthplace, and would be wrapped in swaddling grave clothes in His death place—both symbols of the limitations imposed on His Divinity by taking on a human form.

The Shepherds watching their flocks nearby were told by the angels:

> This is the sign by which you are to know him;
> You will find a child still in swaddling clothes,
> Lying in a manger.

He was already bearing His Cross—the only cross a Babe could bear, that of poverty, exile and limitation. His sacrificial intent already shone forth in the message the angels were singing to the hills of Bethlehem:

> This day, in the city of David,
> A *Saviour* has been born for you,
> No other than the Lord Christ.

Covetousness was already challenged by poverty, while pride was confronted with the humiliation of a stable. The swathing of Divine Power, which otherwise knows no bounds, is often too great a tax upon minds which think only of power in terms of atomic energy. They cannot grasp the idea of divine condescension, or of the "rich becoming poor that through His poverty, we might be rich."

He Whom the angels call the "Son of the most High" descends into the red dust from which we all were born, to be one with weak, fallen man in all things, save sin. And yet it is the swaddling clothes which constitute the "sign". If He Who is Omnipotence had come with thunderbolts, there would have been no sign. There is no "sign" unless something is contrary to nature. The brightness of the sun is no "sign", but an eclipse is. He said that on the last day, His coming will be characterized by "signs in the sun" such as the sun refusing to give its light. Here the Divine Son goes into an eclipse, that only the humble of spirit may recognize Him.

Only two classes of people found the Babe: the Shepherds and the Wise Men. The simple and the learned. They who know they know nothing, and they who know they do not know everything. Never the man with one book; never the man who thinks he knows. Not even God can tell the proud anything. It takes *good will* to find God, and this truth the angels proclaimed from the heavens:

> Peace on earth to men that are God's friends.

As Caryll Houselander put it: "Bethlehem is the inscape of Calvary, just as the snowflake is the inscape of the universe." This is the same idea as that of the poet who said that if he knew the flower in a crannied wall in all its details, he would know "what God and man is." Scientists tell us that the atom prehends within itself the mystery of the solar system. It was not so much that His Birth cast a shadow on His Life, and thus led to His Death; it was rather that the Cross was first, and cast its shadow backward to His Birth. Ordinary mortals go from the unknown to the known and submit themselves to forces beyond their control; hence

Early Life of Christ

we speak of their "tragedy". But He went from the known to the known, from the reason of His Coming, namely to be "Jesus" or "Saviour", to the fulfillment of His Coming, namely the death on the Cross. Hence there was no tragedy in His life, for tragedy implies the unforeseeable, the uncontrollable and the fatalistic. Modern life is tragic when there is no belief in another life and no redemption from guilt. But for this Babe, there are no uncontrollable forces; no submission to fatalistic chains from which there is no escape; but there is an "inscape"—the microscopic manger summarizing a macrocosmic Golgothian cross.

In His First Advent Christ took the name of Jesus or "Saviour"; only in His Second Coming will He take the name of "Judge". Jesus was not a name He had before He, as the Son of God, assumed a human nature; it very properly refers to that which was united to His Divinity, not that which existed from all eternity. Some say "Jesus taught" as some might say "Plato taught," never once thinking that His Name means a *"Saviour from Sin"*. Once He received this name, Calvary was more a part of Him than Washington is related to a President of the United States. The Shadow of the Cross that fell on His cradle, now fell on His naming. Either He lived up to His name, or He did not. If He did not, then He should not be called Jesus or Saviour.

Christ was not two years old when King Herod ordered the killing of the male babies of Bethlehem. It was the first attempt on Christ's life. He faced the sword when a Babe, stones when a man, the Cross at His end. Bethlehem is thus the dawn of Calvary.

A BRIEF LIFE OF CHRIST

The same law that would wind itself around His Apostles and around His followers for centuries, began its first circuit in fresh lives snatched from their mothers' arms—an event now commemorated in the Feast of the Holy Innocents. Upside down on a cross for Peter; a push from a steeple for James, a knife for Bartholomew, a cauldron of oil and a long waiting for John, a sword for Paul—and dashing cutthroats for the babes of Bethlehem.

The world will hate you" is the dark eclipse that hangs over all who are signed with His seal. These Innocents died for the King Whom they never knew, at the hands of an earthly king who should have been their friend. Little lambs, they died for the sake of the Lamb, the prototype of the long procession of martyrs—children who never struggled, but were crowned.

The only acts of Christ's Childhood which are recorded are acts of obedience—to His Heavenly Father and to His earthly parents. The foundation of obedience to man is obedience to God. Delinquency in the young, is the result of delinquency in the parents. The elders who serve not God find the young serve them not. Christ's whole life was submission. He submitted to John's Baptism, though He was exempt from it; He submitted to pay the temple tax, though as the Son of the Father, He was exempt from the tax; He bade His own people submit to Caesar. In being subject to creatures, though He was God, He prepared Himself for that final obedience—obedience to the humiliation of the Cross.

For the next 18 years, after the Three Days Loss,

Early Life of Christ

when He was 12 years of age, He Who carpentered the universe, played the role of a village carpenter, mending flat roofs and fixing the wagons of the farmers. Justin Martyr tells us that in his day—100 years after Christ's death—there were still implements to be seen which were made by His Hands.

Why this long preparation for such a brief ministry of three years?

The reason might very well have been that He waited until the human nature which He had assumed grew in age to full perfection, that He might then offer the perfect sacrifice to His Heavenly Father. The farmer waits until the wheat is ripe before cutting it and subjecting it to the mill. So He would wait until His human nature had reached its most perfect proportions and its peak of loveliness before surrendering it to the hammer of the crucifiers and the sickle of those who cut down the Living Bread of Heaven. The newly born lamb is not offered in sacrifice, nor is the first blush of the new rose cut to pay tribute to a friend. Each thing has its hour of perfection. Since He is the Lamb that sets the hour for the sacrifice, and since He is the Rose that can choose the moment of His cutting, He will wait patiently, humbly and obediently, while He grows in age and grace and wisdom before God and man. Then He will say: "This is your Hour." Thus the choicest wheat and the reddest wine will be the worthiest elements of Sacrifice—the best this world can give for its consecration and its peace.

Temptations

VERY few today believe in the devil. This is exactly what the devil wants. He is always circulating the news of his death. The essence of God is existence, and He defines Himself as: "I am Who am."

The essence of the devil is the lie, and he defines himself as: "I am who am not."

Satan never has to bother with those who do not believe in him; they are already his. But he has a lot of trouble with the saints who are constantly and literally sending him to hell. Satan keeps thousands of devils stationed on monastery walls, but only one in a large city. There are probably some places where the devil sleeps, because he has no work to do.

The devil has used many in our western world to convince us that there is no hell—a thing rather hard to believe, when there is so much evidence for hell around us.

The temptations of man are easy enough to be understood, they always fall into one of three categories: they are either temptations of the flesh, such as lust; or of the mind, such as pride; or of things, such as avarice.

Though man is buffeted all during life by these three temptations, one or the other are more frequent during certain periods of life. It is during youth, that man is most often tempted against purity and inclined to sins of the flesh; in middle age, there is a sublimation of the flesh and the temptations begin to be those of

Temptations

the mind, such as pride and the lust for power; in the autumn of life, temptations very often center about avarice and the possession of material things. Seeing the end of life is near, one strives to compensate for doubts about eternal security or salvation, by piling up the goods of earth as an economic security. It is a common psychological experience, that those who have given way to lust in youth are often those who sin by avarice in their old age.

Good men are not tempted the same way as evil men, nor the Son of God Who became Man, the same way as a good man. The temptations of an alcoholic to "return to his vomit", as Scripture puts it, is not the same as the temptation of a saint to pride, though one is no less real than the other. In order to understand the temptations of Christ, it must be recalled that at the Baptism by John, when He Who had no sins identified Himself with sinners, the heavens opened, and the Heavenly Father declared Christ to be His Beloved Son. Then Our Lord goes to the mountain and fasts for 40 days, after which "He is hungry", in a typical understatement of the Gospel. Satan begins the temptations which revolve around the question: How is He to fulfill His high destiny among men? The problem is to win men. But how! Satan has an idea of how this might by accomplished, namely, by getting Him to forget His name is "Jesus" or "Saviour".

The human flesh, which He had taken upon Himself, was not for leisure, but for battle. Satan saw in Jesus, an extraordinary human being Whom he suspected to be the Messiah and the Son of God. Hence the prefacing of each of the Temptations with the conditional "If". If He were sure He was God, he would not indeed tempt Him. But if He is One Who claims to be God, then he will lead Him into other ways of treating with the sins of mankind than the way that God would choose.

Knowing Our Lord was hungry, Satan pointed down to little black stones that resembled round loaves of bread, and said to Our Lord:

> If thou are the Son of God, bid these
> stones turn into loaves of bread.

The first temptation of Our Blessed Lord was to become a social reformer, and to give bread to the multitudes in the wilderness who were finding nothing but stones. The path of social amelioration without spiritual regeneration, has been the one temptation to which important men of history have most succumbed. But to Him, this would not be adequate service of the Father; there are deeper needs in man than crushed wheat, and there are greater joys than the full stomach.

The evil spirit suggests: "Start with the primacy of the economic! Turn your Churches into social clubs! Forget the supernatural! Does not my Commissar go into classrooms today, and ask children to pray to God for bread? And when their prayers are not answered, my Commissar feeds them? The Dictator gives bread; God does not, because there is no God, there is no soul; there is only the body, pleasure, sex, the animal, and when we die, that is the end."

To that Temptation, Our Lord answers:

Temptations

> Not by bread alone doth man live,
> But by every word that proceedeth
> From the mouth of God.

Our Lord does not deny that men must be fed, or that social justice must be preached, but He asserts that these things are *not first*. He is saying to Satan: "You tempt Me to a religion which would relieve want; you want Me to be a Baker, instead of a Saviour; to be a social reformer, instead of a Redeemer. You are tempting Me away from My Cross, suggesting that I be a cheap leader of people, filling their bellies, instead of their souls; you would have Me begin with security instead of ending with it; you would have Me bring outer abundance, instead of inner holiness. You and your materialists say: 'Man lives by bread alone'. but I say to you: *'Not* by bread alone'. Bread there must be, but remember that even bread gets all of its power to feed from Me. Bread without Me can harm man, and I refuse to hold any theory about security, apart from the Word of God, even though I must go hungry. If I give bread alone, then even dogs shall come to My Banquet. Those who believe in Me must hold that faith, even when they are hungry, starved, weak, in prison, and scourged.

"I am hungry! I have not eaten for forty days, but I refuse to become a mere ethical reformer by catering to the economic and to pleasure and satiety. Say not that I am disinterested in social justice, for I am feeling now the hunger of the world. My stomach groans with the starving, crawling wrecks of humanity. That is why

I fasted, that they can never say God does not know what hunger is. Begone Satan! I am not like some well-fed reformer who says: 'By bread alone'. I refuse any plan which will make men richer without making them holier. Remember! I, Who say: 'Not by bread alone', have not tasted bread in forty days!"

Satan, having failed to win Our Lord away from His Cross and Redemption by turning Him into Commissar promising bread, now turned the attack upon His Spirit and His Soul. Seeing that Our Lord refused to subscribe to the belief that man is a stomach, as he is for some economists, Satan now tempted Him to pride and egotism. As a symbol of that vanity, the devil took Him to a lofty pinnacle of the temple and said to Him: "Cast Thyself down from this to the earth."

Then, quoting Scripture, he continued:

> For it is written He shall give His angels
> Charge concerning Thee, to keep Thee safe,
> And they will hold Thee up with their hands,
> Lest Thou should chance to trip on a stone.

Satan is here saying: "Why take the long and tedious way to win mankind, through the shedding of blood, the mounting of a Cross, through being despised and rejected, when you can take the short cut by a prodigy? You have affirmed Your trust in God. Very well! If You really trust, do something heroic! Prove faith, not by going to a Cross in obedience to God's Will, but by

Temptations

flinging Yourself down. You will never win people to Yourself with sublime truths about Your Divinity preached from church steeples and pinnacles. The masses cannot follow You; they are too far below. Clothe yourself with wonders! Throw Yourself down from the pinnacle and then stop just before you hit bottom! It is the spectacular that people want, not the Divine. People are bored! Relieve the monotony of life and their jaded spirits, but leave their guilty consciences alone!"

The devil's monologue goes on today: "How many times do you read in the press the words: 'Christ says'? Not often. But when do you *not* read: 'Science says'? It is the portents that people want. Science, machines, atomic fission, propaganda, publicity, anything that shows *outer power*—these our young minds crave, and not Your pinnacle truths of sacrifices, grace, forgiveness and penance! If You want to convert minds today, do a miracle: not one that requires faith, but what we call the new miracle, the miracle of science. The children of today, want not Thy miracles, O Christ; not One Who will teach their minds to be subject to God, but one who will teach them to be subject to power. Give up Your sublime truths about the mind needing the faith, the will needing grace, the mind needing hope, the whole being needing God. Power is below! Down in the depths! Jump from your trust in God! Be a magician!"

The answer of Our Lord to Satan then and now is: "Thou shalt not tempt the Lord, thy God."

He means: "You tempt Me, when you admire the

wonders of science, and forget I am the Author of the Universe. Your scientists are proof-readers, not the authors of the Book of Nature; they can come only to the edge of the picture, but not to Me, the Artist Who painted it. You would tempt Me to prove Myself Omnipotent to your feeblest test; you would pull watches on Me and say: 'I challenge you to strike me dead within five minutes.' Know you not that I have mercy on fools? You tempt Me by making atomic bombs explode against My Will and the pleas of My Vicar on earth, and when your cities are shambles, you shriek out: 'Why does God not stop this war?' You tempt Me, saying that I have no power, unless I show it at your beck and call.

"I will never have many followers on the lofty heights of Divine Truth, I know; I will never have the intelligentsia, who are educated beyond their intelligence. I refuse to perform a stunt to win them. It is only when I am lifted on the Cross that I will draw men to Myself; it will be by My sacrifices, and not by science, that I will appeal. I will win followers not with test tubes, but with My blood; not with power, but with Love; not with celestial fireworks, but by the right use of reason and free will. No sign shall be given to this generation but the sign of Jonas, namely, the Divine rising up from below, not the Divine plunging down to hell. It is you, O Satan, who plunges to the depths below. I want men who will believe in Me, even when I do not save them; I will not open the prison doors where My brethren are locked; I want my missionaries and martyrs to love Me in prison as they go

Temptations

singing to their deaths. I never worked a miracle to save Myself! I will work few miracles even for My saints. Begone Satan! Thou shalt not tempt the Lord, thy God."

There is yet one area wherein man can be tempted, and that is outside his body and soul, namely in his relation to the world. "And the devil led Him up on a high mountain, and showed Him all the Kingdoms of the world in a moment of time. 'I will give thee command', the devil said to Him, 'over all these and the glory that belongs to them'. . . ." Then come the most frightening words of Scripture:

> They have all been made over to me,
> And I may give them to whomsoever I please;
> Come then, all shall be thine, if thou wilt fall down
> Before me and worship.

Satan is saying: "You have come, O Christ, to win the world, but the world is mine; I will give it to You, if You will compromise and worship me. Forget Your Cross, Your Divinity, Your Kingdom of Heaven. If You want the world, it is at Your feet. There will be louder Hosannas than Jerusalem ever sang to its Kings; there will be no nails, Golgothas, crowns of thorns and crosses of contradiction. There is no ruler but me. Worship me and the world is Yours."

His language is more modern now, but the temptation is the same. "You will never get ahead in the world unless You accept me. If You build schools to educate children in the ways of God, I will say that You are the enemy of education; if You oppose divorce, fight against the strangulation of the fruits of love, I will say You are 'reactionary.' I will flood the nation with lies, saying that You are the enemy of the State, and I will add to that the bigger lie for fools who will believe it — that You want to dominate the State, and that You are disloyal. Forget heaven, and grace and sacraments and God; no shedding of blood, no martyrdoms, no self-denials are necessary in *my* way. Just worship me *under any name,* I care not what, except do not call me 'devil'. Call me 'power', call me 'religion', provided you leave out Your Divinity, O Christ! Call me 'patriotism', provided You use it to malign those who believe in the spirit; just worship me and the world is Yours."

Our Lord, knowing that those kingdoms could be won only by His suffering and death, said to Satan: "Away with thee, Satan, it is written, 'Thou shalt worship the Lord Thy God, and Him Alone shalt thou serve.' Satan, you want worship, but to worship you is to serve you, and to serve you is slavery. I do not want your world, so long as it has on it the terrible burden of guilt.

"If I had all your kingdoms, all the hearts in them would still long for something you could not give, namely, peace of soul. I do not want your world at your cheap price. I am a revolutionist too, as My Mother sang in her Magnificat. I am in revolt against you. But My revolution is not by the sword thrust outward in imperialism, but inward against sin and all the things that make war. I will first conquer evil in the

Temptations

hearts of men, and then I shall conquer the world. I will conquer your world by going into the hearts of your dishonest tax collectors, your false judges, your Commissars, and I will redeem them from guilt and sin, and send them back clean to their professions. I shall tell them it profits them nothing to win the whole world if they lose their immortal soul. You keep your kingdoms for the moment. Better the loss of all your kingdoms—aye, better the loss of the universe by splitting it with your bombs—than the loss of a single soul! It is the kingdoms of the world that are to be elevated to the Kingdom of God, not the Kingdom of God that is to be dragged down to the level of the kingdoms of the world.

"All I want of this earth is a place large enough to erect a Cross; there I will let you unfurl Me before the cross-roads of your world! I will let you nail Me in the name of the cities of Jerusalem, Athens and Rome, but I will rise from the dead, and you will discover that you, who won the battle, lost the day, as I march with victory on the wings of the morning! Satan, you are asking Me to become anti-Christ. My Divine patience now gives way to Divine indignation. 'Get thee behind Me, Satan'."

Satan asked for a sign that He was the Son of God, and the sign was that He turn the stones into bread. At the marriage Feast of Cana, His Mother asked Him to change the water into wine. Why was it that He refused to a kind of transubstantiation for Satan by changing stones into bread, and why, at the behest of His Mother, did He turn the water into wine?

The occasion was a Marriage Feast to which His Mother had been invited, as well as Himself. He also brought along some of His Disciples, which might have been the reason the wine gave out. In such a wine country, it was only natural that the wine steward appointed for the Feast should be the first to notice the shortage of wine. It happens, however, that the first one who did notice it was the Mother of Our Divine Lord, who went to Him. She uttered a very simple petitionary prayer: "They have no wine." Satan on the mountain top said almost the same thing: "They have no bread." The answer of Jesus to His Mother was: "Woman, what wouldst thou of me? My hour has not yet come."

The next time that He will call His Mother "Woman" will be from the Cross. Then the wine of Cana will be changed into the blood of Calvary. Here is some indication that her relationship with Him is changing. Up to this time, she has been known to the world as the Mother of Jesus; now she would begin to be known as the Mother of all that He would redeem. At the moment Redemption would be completed on the Cross, He would address her again with the title of Universal Motherhood, or "Woman".

Our Blessed Lord never used the word "hour", except in relationship to His Passion and His Death. When Judas betrayed Him, He said: "This is your hour." The night He bade farewell to His Apostles before going into the Garden of Gethsemane, He said:

Temptations

"Father, the hour has come." The "hour" for Him is always an hour of glory through the Cross. He was now telling His Mother that His Hour for announcing His Passion, Death and Resurrection, was not yet at hand. This was a hard decision for any Mother to make, namely, to send a Son into a battlefield with the forces of evil. In the designs of Providence, the hour of His public manifestation had not yet come. And that was why He was hesitant about taking the initiative in the miracle.

She is practically asking Him to advance the Hour in His plan. Moses' prayer stayed the arm of God, as He was about to strike the wayward people; Abraham's prayer would have saved two cities, did He find but a few just men; the plan of the Canaanite woman triumphed over the explicit refusals of Our Lord Himself. Here the plea of His own Mother, expressive of the plea of all humanity for redemption, was sufficient to induce Him to work His first public miracle, to affirm Himself as the Messias and the Saviour of men. She was so certain of her prayer, that she immediately told the wine stewards to fill the water pots, and to bring them to the master of the feast. Our Blessed Lord walked over to them, and in the beautiful language of Richard Crashaw: "The unconscious waters saw their God and blushed." No wonder the guests said to the wine steward: "It is ever the good wine that men set out first, and the worse kind only when all have drunk deep; thou hast kept the good wine till now."

Our Blessed Lord never worked a miracle in order to satisfy His own need, and for that reason He refused to work a miracle to satisfy His own hunger. In every instance when He worked a miracle, it was always as a sign or manifestation of His mission. He would not even work a miracle to save Himself from the Cross. But this miracle is called the first of the signs and wonders that He worked. The world generally gives its best first, and afterwards all its dregs and bitterness, but Christ came to reverse the order and to give the feast after the fast, the Resurrection after a Crucifixion, and the Easter Sunday after a Good Friday.

He did at a marriage feast what He would not do in a desert; He worked in the full gaze of men, what He refused to do before Satan. Satan asked Him to turn stones into bread, in order that He might be an economic Messias; His Mother asked Him to change water into wine that He might begin "His Hour" of Redemption. Satan tempted Him *from* death; Mary "tempted Him" *to* death. Satan would lead Him from the Cross; Mary sent Him on His way. Later on, He would take hold of the bread that Satan said men needed, and the wine which His Mother said the guests needed, and would change them both into the memorial of His Passion and His Death, then He would ask that men renew that memorial, even "unto the consummation of the world." The antiphon of His life continues to ring; everyone else came into the world to live; He came into the world to die.

In the second temptation, Satan took Him to the peak of the Temple in full view of the masses, and asked Him to be an exhibitionist, and to cast Himself down. It was an *ersatz* sacrifice and a false priesthood to which

Temptations

Satan summoned Him, namely, a seeming death in which He would violate the laws of nature and reason.

Our Lord in one of the incidents of His early life, met positively the second temptation of Satan by entering the Temple, and driving out the buyers and the sellers. Gradually, the vendors of articles of sacrifice had pushed themselves closer to the Temple, choking the avenues that led to it until finally, some of them, particularly the sons of Annas, gained entrance to Solomon's porch, there selling doves and cattle and changing money. Every visitor to the feast was obliged to pay half a sheckle to help defray the expenses of the Temple, and since no foreign money could be exchanged, the sons of Annas trafficked in the barter of coins.

There were men with great wicker cages filled with doves, while dealers brought into the Temple, as into the pens of a slaughter house, whole flocks of oxen and bulls and goats and sheep and lambs. The cries of the animals, mixing with the noise of the crowd, suffocated prayer and worship.

Centuries before it had been told of the Messias: "The zeal of thine house hath eaten me up." Though Satan could not make the Saviour jump from the peak of the Temple, the Saviour now moved Himself to His high mission of purifying the Temple by making war on mummeries and hypocrisies and shams.

Satan brought Him to the top of the building, but He entered *into* the Temple. Satan always works on the outside for show, which is the basis of hypocrisy and pride; God always works on the inside, purifying the material that the wings of the spirit may be free.

Taking ropes from the necks of the cattle, He made cords which served as a scourge, with which He drove out the traitors with their sheep and their oxen. Then, with a majestic gesture, He overthrew the tables of the money changers; to the sellers of the gentle doves. He acted gently, saying: "Take these away, do not turn My Father's House into a place of barter."

His eyes darted flames, and His face shone with Divine majesty and the polluters of the Temple, with their troubled consciences, knew in their hearts that He was right. After some time they came back to Him, and asked: "What sign canst Thou show us as Thy warrant for doing this?" They did not reproach Him for what He did, but they asked Him for His title for arrogating to Himself such a power as He claimed when He said to them: "My house shall be known among all the nations for a house of prayer. Whereas you have made it into a den of thieves." Later on He would say that one cannot serve both God and Mammon. Here, as in many other instances, He anticipated His words by divorcing the two. The very fact that He should call the Temple "My Father's House," was also an expression of His unique filial consciousness.

The answer of Our Lord was far beyond their comprehension, as He said to them: "Destroy this Temple, and in three days I will raise it up again." The Gospel immediately adds that "He spoke of the temple of His Body." These words of His would stick in their hearts, and they would repeat them at the trial: "We heard Him say, I will destroy this temple that is made by men's hands, and in three days I will build another,

Temptations

with no hand of man to help me." That is not what He said. Typical of all who pervert words of truth, they wrested it from its true meaning. He spoke of the Temple of His Body which was His humanity.

They immediately asked: How could a temple that had taken 46 years to be rebuilt, be destroyed in a day or two?

What He meant was that the true Temple is the place where God lives. The God-Head was living in His human nature. If, therefore, they would destroy this human nature of His, on the third day He would rise again from the dead, and be God's temple, wherein He would be known and worshipped. The earthly temple ceases to be such, when it becomes the center of mercenary interests. He is the true *shekinah* or glory of the Temple. Though men would nail Him to a Cross, He would still be raised in the hearts and minds of men, and, therefore, would be truly a "Temple not made with hands". The True Temple is the Sacred Body of the Son of God made flesh, in which He is tabernacled amongst us.

The Gospel is quick to add: "When He had risen from the dead, His disciples remembered His saying this, and learned to believe in the Scriptures, and in the words Jesus had spoken."

Though the full meaning is hidden, even from the disciples, there is still an indication that they who were driven out of the temple had a deeper insight into His meaning than they were willing to admit. They brooded over the words, and later on, when they crucified Him as the Temple, and when He lay dead and buried in a rock tomb, they came to Pilate with the remarkable story: "Sir, we have recalled it to memory that this deceiver, while He yet lived, said, I am to rise again after three days." There was more than a passing similarity between that Temple which had destroyed itself with pollution, and the Temple of God which was now before them. Both Temples began in Bethlehem; both were destroyed and raised up again. The Chaldeans destroyed the one, and Zorababel raised it. Mankind would not have God rule over them and destroyed the Temple that God sent. God Himself raised it. Both were consecrated to like uses: the holocaust of obedience, the offering of the body as a reasonable service to the Heavenly Father.

Here, as elsewhere, Our Blessed Lord is proving Himself as the only man who came into this world to die. The Cross was not something that came at the end of His Life. It was something that was sealed upon Him from the very beginning. He said to them: "Destroy", and they said to him: "Crucify". The dome of the Temple, His Head, would be crowned with thorns; the foundation of it, His Sacred Feet, would be riven with nails; its transepts, His Hands, would be laid out as a Cross, and His Holy of Holies, the Heart, would be pierced with a lance. His Crucifixion would not be a punishment inflicted upon Him for antagonizing them; He implied that it was here ordained by His Father, because they had polluted His Father's house. He warned that they would reckon to destroy Him, but they would actually prepare Him only for a short test and the glorious Temple of a risen Body. Later on,

Temptations

St. Paul would say that every Christian is a Temple of the Living God, and such is the basis of his purity and his holiness. This would not have been possible were Christ not already the prototype Temple that was holy with the holiness of God. In Him, the true Temple was the altar of sacrifice and the atonement for sin.

Satan tempted Him to an apparent sacrifice, by tossing Himself from the pinnacle of the Temple, which Our Lord refused to do. But when those who had polluted His Father's House asked Him for a sign, He offered them the sign of the sacrifice on the Cross. Satan told Him to cast Himself down; Our Blessed Lord said that He will be cast down to the obloquy of death, but not because He willed to be an exhibitionist in sacrifice, but because men would demand His Death. Satan, on the peak of the Temple, would tempt Him from a true sacrifice; Our Lord in the Temple pledged Himself to a real sacrifice, but also a Resurrection.

Satan proposed exposing His Temple to possible ruin for the sake of exhibitionism, for the sake of display; Our Lord here exposes the Temple of His Body to real death for the sake of purity. Satan in the wilderness tempted Him to be a wonder worker; in the Temple, He answers that He is a Redeemer. At Cana, He said that He was going to His hour; in the Temple, He says that that Hour of the Cross will lead to His Resurrection. His Public Life will tell the same story.

The Beatitudes

ONE way to make enemies and antagonize people is to challenge the spirit of the world. The world has a spirit, and each age has its peculiar outlook and set of values. One age may be described as "revolutionary", another as "capitalistic", and perhaps another as "'critical". But underlying all of these, the world has certain unanalyzed assumptions which govern conduct. Anyone who challenges these worldly maxims, such as, "you live only once", or "get as much out of life as you can", is bound to make himself unpopular.

This was the first "mistake" of Our Lord, from a worldly point of view. After choosing His 12 Apostles, He delivered what is popularly called: "The Sermon on the Mount", or "The Beatitudes". So often the unthinking say: "The essence of Christianity" is the "Sermon on the Mount". The truth is that the Sermon on the Mount is inseparable from the Mount of Calvary. The day Our Lord preached His Beatitudes, He signed His death warrant. The Sermon on the Mount cannot be separated from the Crucifixion, as day cannot be separated from night.

Sitting down on a mountain top, He opened His mouth and preached:

Blessed are the poor in spirit;
    the kingdom of heaven is theirs.
Blessed are the patient; they shall inherit the land.

The Beatitudes

Blessed are those who mourn; they shall be comforted.
Blessed are those who hunger and thirst for holiness; they shall have their fill.
Blessed are the merciful; they shall obtain mercy.
Blessed are the clean of heart; they shall see God.
Blessed are the peace-makers; they shall be counted the children of God.
Blessed are those who suffer persecution in the cause of right; the kingdom of heaven is theirs.
Blessed are you, when men revile you, and persecute you, and speak all manner of evil against you falsely, because of me.
Be glad and lighthearted, for a rich reward awaits you in heaven.

To be "blessed" means to be happy.

Poor in spirit: "Poor" does not mean indigent. To be poor in spirit is to be conscious of one's spiritual poverty, to blush at one's own defects, to have a deep sense of nothingness before God, and to be resigned before the beneficent Hand of Providence. The foundation of all spiritual happiness is to be conscious before God of one's emptiness or one's need, like the publican smiting his breast. Poverty of spirit is the very antithesis of the worldly doctrine of self-sufficiency.

The patient: The patient bow to the rod of affliction, and bear injury meekly; in prosperity, they are thankful, and in adversity, they are resigned. Patience is meekness, which is opposed to anger, resentment, and retaliation. It is a consequence of the first Beatitude, for he who has learned the depth of his own weakness, will not be so ready to strike others, but will rather approach them with clemency. The land they will possess is not landed property; the Beatitude rather means that they can now enjoy the earth as a stepping stone to life eternal. The meek person is never disturbed by the fact that someone else owns something; possession to him is not an annoyance, but a pleasure which he takes as it comes; therefore, he enjoys the earth. Meek men in the Old Testament, like Caleb and Josue, inherited the Promised Land.

Those who mourn: Those who mourn are not the weepers from discontent, but those who feel the sorrows and the sins of the world as their own. The world regards sorrow as disaster; Our Lord looks upon it as the darkness that heralds the dawn. The sorrow here is not so much physical as spiritual, that is, for *sin* rather than the consequences of sin. Once the soul looks into its own past, and sees there its multiplied rejections of Divine Love, it cannot help but mourn. This contrition is the condition of moral progress and the pathway to true comfort and peace of soul.

Those who hunger and thirst: They are those who so yearn for holiness, which is abandonment to the Will of God in all things, that they would die rather than commit a single sin. The hunger and thirst here is not physical, but spiritual; it is not just an inner dissatisfaction with human prescriptions, but rather a yearning to attain holiness and righteousness which is conformity to the Will of God. Swine are satisfied with husks, but not the soul of immortal man. It is the *desire* of holiness that is blessed; the achievement and perfection of it is on God's side. We receive it, but we do not *create* it. All the cups of earth of which we drink are empty, as regards the thirst of the soul. Only God can fill both the cup and him who drinks.

The merciful: The merciful pardon others and obtain pardon; because they need mercy, they show it; while hating the sin, they love the sinner and say: "Father, forgive." Selfishness is hell; mercy is heaven. The world gives back as a mirror what we put into it. As we show mercy, we receive it; as we forgive others, we receive forgiveness. But the Beatitudes do not assume that we will receive mercy because we show it, but rather, because we have received forgiveness of our sins from God, we will be forgiving others. Mercy is a *consequence*, not the *cause* of receiving God's Mercy. Our mercy then becomes the effort to *redeem*, but this cannot be done without sacrifice, as the Life of Christ reveals.

The clean of heart: The pure of heart are those who control all lusts, not as a denial of love, but as a guarding of it until the body can be used as God wills it to be used. The "seeing of God" which is the privilege of the pure, does not mean with human eyes, but with the eye of the spirit. Carnal lusts are at enmity with the spirit. Bad behaviour keeps as many from seeing God as does ignorance. Under the slavery of sex, a mind sees nothing straight. As clouds hide the sun, so habits of an unclean mind hide God. Impurity is a cataract on the eye of the soul. There is a reciprocity between sight and seeing the heavens, between a clean heart and seeing God.

The peace-makers: Peace is not the absence of war, but the tranquility of order. Order is the subordination of senses to reason, body to soul; reason to faith, the whole personality to God. Peace is not automatic; it is *made*. He is no peacemaker who has no scourge in his hands against evil, whose love does not hate sin, and who is incapable of righteous indignation. Peace is based not on expediency, but on justice. The peacemaker must fight without ever ceasing to be love. Such peace is first not in nations, but in souls. A peaceful world comes not by legislation, but by inner regeneration. Only he who has the peace of God in his own soul, can give it to others. God hates "peace" in those who are destined for war, and we are all destined for war against sin and evil. Those who make such peace shall be the children of God, the Prince of Peace.

The eighth beatitude about the persecuted, is the summary of the preceding seven. The persecuted are those who know that to follow Christ is to be hated; hogs will say they are dirty; goats will say they smell; wolves will accuse them of stealth. But abuse, scourges, jails, blood-martyrdoms, all these must be accepted as a blessing which bears witness to Christ. The Preacher on the Mount is not summoning men to ease and comfort, but to suffering for His Name's sake.

In these beatitudes, Our Divine Lord takes those eight flimsy catchwords of the world: 'Security', 'Revenge', 'Laughter', 'Popularity', 'Getting even', 'Sex', 'Armed

The Beatitudes

Might', and 'Comfort' and turns them upside down. To those who say: "Strike it rich", He says, "Blessed are the poor in spirit". To those who say: "Don't let him get away with it", He says: "Blessed are the patient". To those who say: "Laugh and the world laughs with you", He says: "Blessed are those who mourn". To those who say: "Never restrain your instincts", He says: "Blessed are the clean of heart". To those who say: "Become popular by flattery", He says: "Blessed are you when men revile you and persecute you". To those who say: "In time of peace, prepare for war", He says: "Blessed are the peace-makers".

The cheap cliches around which movies are written and novels composed, He scorns. He proposes to burn what they worship, to conquer sex instead of explaining man by it as does Freud, to tame economic lusts instead of sending minds to Adam Smith or to Karl Marx. All the modern ideas that say happiness depends on 'self-expression', 'license', 'having a good time', or 'eat, drink and be merry for tomorrow you die', He scorns because they bring mental disorders, unhappiness, false hopes, fears and anxieties. The new paganism, like its ancient masters—Seneca, Marcus Aurelius, Epictetus—gives us nothing but cascading platitudes, which take man as he *is*. Christ talks of what man is to *become,* and through no energy of his own, but through His Grace. Nowhere do you find Him speaking those cheap platitudes posted on church lawns: "Leave the world better than you find it." But you do hear Him say: "What doth it profit a man if he gain the whole world and lose his soul?"

A BRIEF LIFE OF CHRIST

Those who would escape the impact of the Beatitudes say that Our Divine Saviour was a creature of His time, but not of ours, and that, therefore, His Words do not apply to us. He was not a creature of His time, or of any time, but we are; Mohammed belonged to his time: hence he said a man could have concubines in addition to four wives at one time. Mohammed belongs even to *our* time, because moderns say that a man can have many wives if he drives them in tandem style, one after another. But Our Lord did not belong to His days, any more than He belonged to ours. To marry one age is to be a widow in the next. Because He suited no age, He was the model for all ages. He never used a phrase that depended on the social order in which He lived; His Gospel was no easier then than it is now. As He put it: "Heaven and earth must disappear sooner than one jot, one flourish should disappear from the law; it must all be accomplished."

The key to the Sermon on the Mount is the way He used two expressions: One was: "You have heard", the other was the short emphatic word, "But". When He said: "You have heard", He reached back to what human ears heard for centuries and still hear from ethical reformers—all those rules and codes and precepts which were half measures between instinct and reason, between local customs and the highest ideals. When He said: "You have heard", He included the Mosaic Law, Buddha with his eight-fold way, Confucius with his rules for being a gentleman, Aristotle with his natural happiness, the broadness of the Hindus, John Dewey, H.G. Wells, Bertrand Russell and all

The Beatitudes

the humanitarian groups of our day, who have translated some of the old codes into English and call them a new way of life. Of all these compromises, He said: "You have heard".

"*You have heard* that it was said, Thou shalt not commit adultery." Moses had said it, pagan tribes suggest it; primitive people respected it. Then came the terrible and awful BUT: "But I tell you. . . ." "But I tell you that he who casts his eye on a woman so as to lust after her, has already committed adultery with her in his own heart." Our Lord went into the will, and laid hold of thought, and branded even *the desire* as a sin. If it was wrong to do a certain thing, it was wrong to think about that thing. He was saying: "Away with your hygiene which tries to keep hands clean after they have stolen, and bodies free from disease after they have ravished another." *He* goes into the depths of the heart and brands even the intention a sin. He does not wait for the evil tree to bear evil fruits. He would prevent the very sowing of the evil seed. Wait not until your hidden sins come out as psychoses and neuroses and compulsions. Get rid of them at their sources. Repent! Purge! Evil that can be put into statistics, or that can be locked in jails, is too late to remedy.

Looking forward to our nation, with one divorce for every four marriages, Christ affirms that when a man marries a woman, he marries both her body and her soul; he marries the whole person. If he gets tired of the body, he may not thrust her body away for another, since he is still responsible for her soul. So He thunders: "You have heard." In that expression, He summarized the jargon of every decaying civilization. "You have heard—Get a divorce; 'God does not expect you to live without happiness'." Then came the BUT: "But I tell you, that the man who puts away his wife, makes an adulteress of her, and whoever marries her after she has been put away, commits adultery." What matters if the body is lost? The soul is still there, and that is worth more than the thrill a body can give, more even than the universe itself. He would keep men and women pure, not from contagion, but from desire; to imagine a betrayal is in itself a betrayal. So He thundered: "What God then, has joined, let not man put asunder." No man! No judge! No nation!

Next Christ laid hold of all those social theories which say that sin is due to environment, to Grade B milk, to insufficient dance halls, to not enough spending money. Of them all, He says: "You have heard." Then comes the BUT: "But I tell you." He affirms that sins, selfishness, greed, adultery, crime, theft, bribery, political corruption, come from man himself. The offenses result from our own will, and not from our glands; we cannot excuse our lust because our grandfather had an Oedipus complex, or because we inherited an Electra complex from our grandmother. Sin, He says, is conveyed to the soul sometimes through the body, and our body is moved by will. In war against all false self-expressions, He thunders out His recommendations of self-operation: "Cut it off." "Cut it out." "And if thy right eye is the occasion of falling, cut it out and cast it away from thee; better to lose one part of thy body than to have the whole cast into hell. . . . And if thy right hand is

The Beatitudes

the occasion of falling, cut it off and cast it away from thee; better to lose one of thy limbs than to have the whole body cast into hell." Men will cut off their legs and arms to save the body from gangrene or poisoning. But here, Our Lord transfers circumcision of the flesh to circumcision of the heart, and advocates letting out the life blood of our beloved lusts and hewing our passions to tatters, rather than be separated from the love of God which is in Him, Christ Jesus.

Next, He talks of our modern attitude of revenge, hatred, violence, expressed in those sayings of everybody: "Get even", "Sue him", "Don't be a fool"—He knows them all, and of all of them He says: "You have heard that it was said, 'an eye for an eye and a tooth for a tooth'." Then comes the awful BUT: "But I tell you, that you should not offer resistance to injury; if a man strikes thee on thy right cheek, turn the other cheek also towards him; if he is ready to go to the law with thee over thy coat, let him have it and cloak with it; and if he compels thee to attend him on a mile's journey, go two miles with him of thy own accord."

Why turn the other cheek? Because hate multiplies like a seed. If someone preaches hate and violence to ten men in a row, and tells the first man to strike the second, and the second to strike the third, the hatred will envelop all ten. The only way to stop this hate, would be for one man, say the fifth in line, to turn his other cheek. Then the hatred ends. It is never passed on. Absorb violence for the sake of your Saviour, Who absorbs your sins and dies for them. The Christian law is that the innocent shall suffer for the guilty.

A BRIEF LIFE OF CHRIST

And with these sayings, He is throwing down the gauntlet to all those who try to make the innocent guilty with their mock trials. He would have us do away with adversaries, because when no resistance is offered, the adversary is conquered by a superior moral power; such love prevents the infection of the wound of hate. To endure the bore who inflicts you for a week; to write a letter of kindness to the man who calls you dirty names; to offer gifts to the man who would steal from you; never to answer back with hatred the man who lies and says you were disloyal to your country, or tells the worse lie that you are against freedom—these are the hard things which Christ came to teach, and they no more suited His time than they do ours. They suit only the heroes, the great men, the saints, the holy men and women, who will be the salt of the earth, the leaven in the mass, the elite among the mob, the kind who will transform the world. If we do not find certain people lovable, He bids us put love into them and they will be lovable. Why are we ever lovable—if it be not that God put love into us?

The Sermon on the Mount is so much at variance with all that our world holds dear, that the world will crucify anyone who tries to live up to its values; because Christ preached them, He had to die. Calvary was the price He paid for the Sermon on the Mount. Only mediocrity survives. Those who call black, black, and white, white, are sentenced for intolerance. Only the grays live.

Let Him Who says: "Blessed are the poor in spirit", come into the world that believes in the primacy of the

The Beatitudes

economic; let Him stand in the market place where Marx and Lenin say that man lives for collective profit, or where monopolistic capitalism says man lives for individual profit. He will be so poor that during life, He will have nowhere to lay His head, and a day will come when He will die without anything of economic worth. In His last hour, He will be so impoverished, that they will strip Him of His garments, and even give Him a stranger's grave for His burial.

Let Him come into the world in which Nietzsche proclaims his gospel of the strong, advocates hating our enemies, and condemns Christian virtues as the "soft" virtues, and say to that world: "Blessed are the patient"—and He will one day feel the scourges of the strong barbarians laid across His back. He will see them take a sickle and cut the grass from a hill on Calvary, and then use a hammer to pinion Him to a Cross to test the patience of One Who awaits eternity.

Let Him come into our world with its divorce courts, its psychoanalysts ridiculing the idea of sin as morbidity, a world of progressive educators who deny discipline for the young, and preach to that world: "Blessed are they who mourn" for their sins, and they will blindfold Him and mock Him as a fool. They will take His body and scourge it until His bones can be numbered; and they will crown His head with thorns, until He begins to weep not salt tears, but crimson beads of blood, as they laugh at the weakness of Him Who will not come down from the Cross.

Let Him come into a world that believes in the philosophy of pragmatism and relativism, a world which denies Absolute Truth, which says that right and wrong are only questions of point of view, that we must be broadminded about virtue and vice, and let Him say to them: "Blessed are they who hunger and thirst after holiness", that is, after the Absolute, after the Truth which I am, and outside of which there is no other; and they will, in their broadmindedness, give the mob the choice of Him or Barrabas, will crucify Him with thieves and try to make the world believe that God is no different from a batch of robbers who are His bedfellows in death.

Let Him come into the world of Sartre, who says that my neighbor is hell, that all that is opposite me is nothing, that the ego alone matters, that my will is supreme law, that what I decide is good, that I must forget others and think only of myself, and say to them: "Blessed are the merciful", and He will find that He will receive no mercy; they will open five rivers of blood out of His body, they will pour vinegar and gall into His thirsting mouth, and even after His death, be so merciless as to lunge a spear into His Sacred Heart.

Let Him come into a world which tries to interpret man in terms of sex; which seasons the novel, movie and television show with an attack on the sanctity of marriage, which says that a marriage endures only until the glands tire; that one may unbind what God binds, and unseal what God seals, and say to them: "Blessed are the pure", and He will find Himself hanging naked on a Cross that defies their crazy affirmation that purity is abnormal, that the virgins are neurotics and that their carnality is right.

The Beatitudes

Let Him come into a world of Vishinskys and Molotovs, who believe with Lenin that one must resort to every manner of chicanery and duplicity in order to conquer the world, who carry doves of peace with stomachs full of bombs, and say to them: "Blessed are the peace-makers", or "Blessed are they who eradicate sin that there may be peace", and He will find Himself surrounded by the comrades of the Vishinskys and Molotovs, as they make the greatest war this world of ours ever saw: the war against the Son of God; after His death, they will set a guard about His grave to prevent a Resurrection, something they would not expect even from a Lenin.

Let Him come into a world that believes personality should be manipulated; that our whole life should be geared to flattering and influencing people for the sake of utility and popularity, and say to them: "Blessed are ye when men hate you and persecute you and revile you", and He will find Himself without a friend in the world, an outcast on a hill, with mobs shouting His death and His flesh hanging from Him like purple rags.

The Beatitudes cannot be taken alone; they are not ideals; they are hard facts and realities, inseparable from the Cross of Calvary. Many men go on repeating them, but very few of us are willing to live them! It is easy to be self-expressive, all one has to do is avoid repressing the *id;* it is easy to be a liberal, all one has to do is espouse no cause as sacred, except the right to be free from discipline and the Eternal Law of God; it is easy to be a social reformer, and to take care of other people's consciences; it is easy to be a milk and water

Christian who quotes the Sermon on the Mount, and forgets the Christ Who died for it. It is easy to be an intellectual and to sneer at the humble. It is easy to love those who love us.

But it is hard to love those who hate us, to pluck out one's eyes and cut off arms to prevent sinning; it is hard to be clean on the inside when the passions clamor for satisfaction on the outside; to forgive those who would put us to death; to overcome evil with good; to bless those who curse us, to stop mouthing freedom until we have justice, truth and love of God in our hearts as the condition of freedom; to live in the world and still keep oneself unpolluted from the world; to deny ourselves sometimes legitimate pleasures, like cigarettes, cocktails, movies and luxuries, in order to help missionaries feed the leprous, fill the empty rice bowls and renew hungry hearts with the grass of God; to see that all our clap-trap about the brotherhood of man is meaningless unless we all have the same God as Father! What kind of men would we be if we did not know Our Father?—a race of illegitimate children. To strive not to be like the rest of men, but to be Perfect as the Heavenly Father is perfect—this is the only new thing in the world, but there are very few who are willing to try it. Christianity has not failed; but we have failed the Christ who said: "Take up your cross and follow Me."

Public Life and Passion

OVER thirty times during His Life, Jesus Christ spoke of a *must* about His sufferings and death. Those who quarrel and bicker about who put Him to death are very much off center. Our Lord was under no outer compulsion; He was not a victim of circumstances beyond His control; He was not a devotee of the world's highest values, like a soldier dying on a battlefield; He was not a martyr for a great cause; not a moral teacher Whom the mediocre slew because they could not stand the moral lashings of His purity. He went to death not because of the plotting of evil men, nor because He was a victim of circumstances quite beyond His control, nor because of the power of the Roman Empire. True indeed, the stage was set by evil men, but Our Lord always presents Himself as One Who took charge of the plot. He went to death in obedience to His Father, with Whom He is one in nature! "The Father and I are one".

Buddha came into this world to live, so did Socrates, so did Confucius, so did Moses and the Prophets. However, there was One Person Who came into the world to die, and that was the Eternal Galilean, Jesus Christ.

The Cross came at the end of His Life, from a *time* point of view, but it was hovering over the crib from an intentional point of view.

There is a maxim in philosophy: "What is first in intention is last in execution". A young man decides to become a doctor. But the intention is perhaps 12 years or more before he receives his M.D. In like manner, the Cross was first in intention in the earthly life of Christ, but the last in execution. Our lives are lived forward; *His life was lived backward.* The Cross was the reason for the crib and His teaching, not His crib and His teachings the reason for His Cross.

Nothing is more beautiful in His character than the way He prepared His Apostles for that unpalatable lesson of seeming defeat as the condition of victory. How slow they were to understand the story of why He *must* suffer, but with what infinite patience He instructed them. He took two steps in unfolding the mystery of His death and why it was necessary:

> 1. An occasional reference to the need of sacrifice, until they were convinced by prophecies and miracles that He was the Son of God.
>
> 2. A bold announcement of the Cross after Peter confessed: "Thou art the Christ, the Son of the Living God."

1. Though He knew from the beginning that His Father so loved the world that He sent Him into it to redeem men from their sins, nevertheless, He could not tell this to His Apostles without arousing their prejudice or destroying their feeble faith. Instead of saying that He would sacrifice Himself, He began by telling them that they should sacrifice themselves. For example, when He was seen in the company of publicans, some of the "nice people" lifted their eyebrows,

Public Life and Passion

but He explained to His disciples: "I came not to save the just, but the sinners." To heal men of sin is a greater manifestation of Power than to exterminate sinners by punishment. He did not tell them at that moment, how this was to be accomplished, but only that such was His purpose.

Next, He warned them that as a result of their companionship with Him, they too would have to suffer. "The servant is not above the Master." He even tells them they are to consider themselves "blessed" when "men shall hate you... and cast out your name as evil". This was a strange forecast to give disciples, namely because they followed Him they would have missiles thrown at them. Before Him and since many have preached that if you are good, you will be prosperous; Jesus tells them that if they are good, they will be persecuted: "You shall be hated by all men for My Name's sake".

He hoped they, being reasonable men, would draw inferences from such warnings as: "Fear ye not them that kill the body, and are not able to kill the soul". Why should He Who had the power to raise the dead, and lift up limbs long palsied with disease and death, now tell them not to fear those who would torture their bodies? Would His body he tortured? Was He bidding them to do something from which He would exempt Himself by His power? They knew the soul was worth more than the body, but why speak of their bodies being killed? Would they die as martyrs?

The conclusion was inevitable: He was bidding them to a life of sacrifice because He would be sacrificed. He did not yet say that He would offer Himself for the sinners of the world; rather, He said because His sacrifice was a Divine "must" laid upon Him by love, they must be prepared for the same maltreatment, because they were His servants.

Despite His patience in educating His followers, they did not grasp the lesson. The disproportion between His mind and theirs was infinitely greater than Shakespeare teaching the alphabet to a three-year-old child. Added to this was the "scandal" of the Cross, for what mysterious faith was this He was giving them which would provoke so much of the world to hate?

2. About the middle of His public life, the Apostles who followed Him saw the opposition against Him grow. Groups that despised one another united in one great phalanx of conspiracy, determined if possible to alienate the affections of the common people who marveled at His works.

Leaving Bethsaida, He enters the half-pagan city of Caesarea-Philippi, where there was a statue to the god Pan. While there, the culminating point of His earthly ministry occurred. When He had finished His prayer, He beckoned His Apostles to Him and asked them the most important question He ever asked: "Whom do men say that I am?" Perhaps the reason He asked the popular judgment of men concerning Him was to reveal to them how much in the eyes of the public He had failed. "Men", they said, "thought Him to be Elias, Jeremias, John the Baptist, or one of the Prophets."

Then He asked: "Whom do *you* say that I am?" The

Public Life and Passion

popular answer had been full of contradictions. Now the elect, the spiritual aristocracy was asked, but they did not answer.

One man then steps forward, Peter, who answered: "Thou art the Christ, the Son of the Living God." Our Blessed Lord answers:

> Blessed art thou, Simon son of Jona;
> It is not flesh and blood,
> It is My Father in Heaven
> That has revealed this to thee.

He was telling Peter that He did not know this of and by himself, but because of a revelation of His Father. It was faith that made him stand alone and apart from the world, and above all of its judgments. Our Lord then makes Peter "the rock upon which I will build My Church".

But this is only half the story. Now that Our Lord was known to be what He is, the Messias, the Son of the Eternal Father, He prepared them for the second lesson: He is the suffering Messias spoken of by Isaias and the other prophets, "the Lamb led to slaughter", "the One on Whom are laid the transgressions of us all".

The Apostles had to learn the first lesson thoroughly before they could face boldly the second lesson, namely, that He Who is the God-Man should suffer and die. The "must" of which He spoke when He was 12 years of age, is now clearly revealed: He *must* die because He *would* save. The Divine Messias must be a rejected Messias, and a rejected Messias must be a slain Messias.

A BRIEF LIFE OF CHRIST

> From that time onwards Jesus began to
> Make it known to His disciples
> That He must go up to Jerusalem, and there,
> With much ill-usage from the priests
> And elders and scribes must he put to death,
> And rise again on the third day.

The work of His Cross can be understood only in the light that He is the Father's Son. He tells His Apostles now what He will tell them after His Resurrection, that it was "fitting that the Son of Man suffer", that the necessity of suffering comes not from rejection by elders, chief priests and scribes, nor is it due to the accumulation of popular prejudice. The web in which He is caught on Calvary's Hill will not be spun by the hands of spider men. The Divine *must* comes from two sides: the obedience to His Father's Will, and His love of men. The first pointed Him to the Cross, the second nailed Him there and kept Him there, despite the cries to "come down and we will believe", until the work was finished.

Peter did not understand the Divine *must,* for he "rebuked" Our Lord for suggesting that He would suffer. It was at this point that Our Blessed Lord called him "Satan". Peter had done exactly the same thing that Satan had done in the wilderness, namely, tried to turn Him away from the Cross, and make Him a political Messias Who would give belly-bread instead of soul-bread. Our Lord implied that suggesting the merely human way out of a Divine Mission is identical with being diabolical. Then He told Peter that what he

Public Life and Passion

said savored not of the things of God, but of the things of men.

Jesus then tells them that His law should be their law: A Good Friday is the prelude to an Easter Sunday. But there is this difference. He is under a Divine Mandate of the Father to which His Will is identified perfectly. But, they are free to choose. Hence, He said He "must" suffer, but as for them: *"If* any will follow Me, let him take up his cross and follow Me". This was one of the conditions of discipleship. They knew what a cross was, for they had often seen the Romans execute criminals on the hills outside the city.

Now He says: "Whosoever does not take his cross and come after Me, cannot be My disciple". But He also consoles them by saying that the same suffering servant who mounts a Cross will one day come attended by the hosts of heaven to judge every man according to his works. The cross is only a means, not an end; it is the prelude to the crown. From now on, He spoke openly of His Death, never mentioning His Cross without His Resurrection, but they could not understand either clearly until Pentecost and the coming of the Spirit.

Another very remarkable reference to His Divine Mission of saving men from sin was manifested to His Apostles on the Mount of Transfiguration. Three major scenes of His Life took place on mountains: the Mount of the Beatitudes, the Mount of the Transfiguration and the Mount of Calvary. All three hills are related one to the other. The first was the proclamation of a message that would antagonize the world. The second was the revelation of His Glory through death; and the third, the supreme act of love, the ransom of men. The incident took place about a week after Peter had confessed that He was the Son of the Living God.

Our Lord took with Him three Apostles: Peter, James and John. Peter the "rock", James the one destined to be the first Apostle Martyr, and John the visionary of the future glory of the Apocalypse. Undoubtedly, He chose these three because they most needed strength for the hour of trial.

On the mountain top, He became transfigured, His face shining as the sun, and His garments becoming white as snow. While there, Moses and Elias conversed with Him: Moses, the publisher of the Law, and Elias, the chief of the Prophets. His Sacred Person seemed to be living with the Light of Glory flashing through the threads of His earthly raiment. It was not so much a light that was shining from without, as a light coming from the essential beauty of the Godhead within. It was not a miracle, but a witness of the abiding presence of Christ's Divinity. The glory that shone around Him as the Temple of God, was not something with which He was outwardly invested, but rather a natural expression of the inherent loveliness of "Him Who came down from Heaven".

The wonder was not this momentary radiance around Him: it was rather that at all other times, it was repressed. As Moses, after communing with God, put a veil over his face to hide it from the people of Israel,

Public Life and Passion

so Christ had veiled His Glory in humanity. But for this brief moment, He turns it aside so that men may see it; the outgoing of these rays was the transitory proclamation to every human eye of the Son of Righteousness. In one brief moment, Heaven seemed to enshrine the earthly life, which was the Glory of God.

Peter expressed his happiness that they were there. Attempting to capture this glory which was transient, he suggested building three tents or tabernacles there: one for Moses, one for Elias, and one for Christ. Just one week before, Peter was trying to find a way to glory without the Cross. Peter now once more attempts indirectly to dissuade Our Lord from going to Jerusalem to be crucified, and thus becomes the spokesman of all those who would enter into glory without purchasing it by self-denial and sacrifice. Peter, with his impetuous character, feels that the glory which God brought down from the Heavens could be tabernacled among men, without ever purchasing it by the Cross of Calvary. But while Peter would have a glory without the Cross, Our Lord is speaking to Moses and Elias of His Death. "And they spoke of the Death which He was to achieve at Jerusalem".

His death on the Cross would not be a surprise or an accident, but a work which He came to accomplish and which would be a fulfillment of both the Law and the Prophets. In the moment of His greatest glory, He draws aside the effulgence of the Divine which is really His and shows Himself speaking of His death, of His scourging and crowning with thorns and Crucifixion. At a moment when He seemed to be least a Man of

Sorrows, He converses with the Law and the Prophets of the impending tragedy. The Divine Face which was now shining so brightly with the Light of God, must be smitten and spit upon. The gossamer of light which now surrounds Him would have to be exchanged for being stripped naked on a Hill. The Sacred Brow which glistened with Heavenly Glory, would have to be studded with thorns, woven by soldiers cursing the thorns that had so lightly pricked their thumbs.

While the Apostles were standing at what seemed to be the very vestibule of Heaven, a cloud formed overshadowing them:

> And a voice came from the cloud
> This is My Beloved Son;
> To Him, then, listen.

When God sets up a cloud, it is a manifest sign that there are bonds we cannot break. At His Baptism, the Heavens were opened and now, at the Transfiguration, they open again to install Him in His office as Mediator, and to distinguish Him from Moses and the Prophets. It was Heaven itself that was sending Him on His mission of saving men, not the perverse will of men.

The purpose of the Transfiguration was also to strengthen His Apostles for the impending blow of His death. By itself, this show of glory could have brought His earthly life to a fitting climax, if there were no sin. His own spotless life deserved the crown without the cross, the glory without the suffering. Thus thought Peter, too. But neither Peter, nor James nor John could

Public Life and Passion

probably have endured the shock of defeat, had they not first been strengthened by the sight of Jesus in His glory—a forecast of what He would be after the Resurrection. It was these three to whom special revelations would be made after His Resurrection. This perfect knowledge of His future glory alone could sustain them for Calvary. Then when John at the foot of the Cross, would hear Him say: "My God! My God! Why hast Thou abandoned Me?," he could recall the assuring words from the Father in Heaven: "This is My Beloved Son."

Another interesting reference to His act of ransom was a parable that is almost autobiographical, namely, the parable of the dishonest tenants. The rulers had just been questioning Our Lord as to the authority by which He acted. The position that they took was that they were representatives and guardians of the people, and, therefore, they must prevent the people from being misled. Our Lord answers them in a parable, showing them the kind of guardians and guides they were. He points out several steps in the planting of a vineyard: it is furnished with all the necessary appliances, has a wall around it, a wine press and a tower. God had enclosed His people with His own hands, and prepared them to be a fruitful vine. The letting out of the vineyard to those who tended it, meant the commitment to His own people of responsibility. This commitment began with Abraham, who had been called out of the land of Ur, and with Moses, who gave his people commandments, and the worship of the true God by which they emerged from the wilderness of barbarism.

The next scene is one in which the owner of the vineyard claims the returns, namely, fidelity and love of God. Our Lord describes that the messengers who are the prophets were subjected to cruel treatment and often murder. The more God pleaded with them, the more bitter they became.

Under figure of speech He is saying that a special Providence which had protected and defended His people against all enemies, should have prompted them to have been grateful. Then Jesus draws the last arrow from the quiver of the parable and said of the owner of the vineyard, Who is His Heavenly Father:

> He still had one messenger left,
> His only Beloved Son,
> Him He sent to the last of all;
> They will have reverence, He said,
> For My Son.

He sets Himself apart from the servants or the prophets and tells His auditors that He comes from the owner of the vineyard, God Himself. Christ here presents Himself as God's last appeal to the sinful world, a supreme gift of infinite love. The Father hopes that His Son will be counted as standing for Himself, and the gratitude and affection and reverence that is due to Him, will be shown to His Son. And Our Lord, continuing the parable, says:

> But the vine-dressers said among themselves,
> This is the heir, come, let us kill Him,

Public Life and Passion

And then His inheritance will be ours.

So they look Him and killed Him
And cast Him out of the vineyard.

Our Blessed Lord under this symbol, reminds His hearers of the melancholy fact that He will receive but little reverence from mankind. Rebuffs and injuries and insults would be the greeting extended the Beloved Son of the Heavenly Father.

Within three days of the telling of the story, it came true. The accredited keepers of His vineyard who cast Him out of the city onto a hill that was used as a dump, contrived to put Him to death. Man can thwart God's purpose at least for a time, but as Augustine said: "They slew Him that they might possess, and because they slew, they lost."

Later, He tells His enemies that they will not come to recognize Who He is, until He has been crucified.

When you have lifted up the Son of Man,
You will recognize that it is Myself you look for,
And that I do not do anything of My own impulse,
But speak as My Father has instructed Me to speak.

Only after the Crucifixion will they know what He spoke. The Crucifixion would not be the last in the series of failures. It would be the revelation of His glory, and would cause a reaction in men's minds concerning Him, when they finally had placarded Him outside of the city's gates. The Cross and the Crown would be the truth to the most obtuse and bigoted, "that I am that what I say I am". The forecast here is the conversion of His enemies as a result of His Death and Resurrection.

When a man is leading a great social movement, the worst thing that can happen to him is to die. But He said the cross is the condition of drawing men unto Himself. If He were merely a man, the Cross to Him would be His scaffold. But as the Eternal Son of the Father, it would be a throne. If He were a martyr, His Death would be defeat; but if He is God, it will be a victory. If He were a man, the Cross would be a repulsion; being God, it would be a world-wide attraction.

If the message that He taught had come only from a man, its chief emphasis would have been placed by His followers not on the Cross, but on the Mount of Beatitudes. It is singular that those who miss His Divine message are always the ones that insist upon the Mount of Beatitudes. If He were only a man, Christians would have drawn a veil over those hours of Calvary, and would have stressed solely the wisdom of the Teacher and the majesty of the King. Instead of this, true Christians boast of that which must have appeared as a failure to human eyes.

If Our Lord had come to this earth and had been fenced in by all the comforts of life, and after teaching the true theory of pain, had died on a soft bed, He might have been honored as a great Teacher, but He would never have drawn men to Himself. Nowhere does He say: "Obey a code", but rather, "Follow Me". Everything said about His sufferings and death revealed

Public Life and Passion

that He voluntarily committed Himself to some great task which his Father had given Him, and that task was first and foremost the delivery of mankind from the burden of sin. His death was as the fulfillment of Divine purpose in which His will was One with that of the Father; His words and acts are those of One who knows what He is doing and why He must do it.

Men are called to participate in the fruits of His death. Man's attitude is not to be passive toward this redemption. The obedience to His Father's Will is His own, but since He presents it as the Son of Man, it is also a representative obedience. It is the obedience which men ought to offer to God, and which they should offer, did they fulfill the obligations of sonship. Representing men, He offers that obedience in their name and for their sake, with the intention that they should identify themselves with it, and so offer themselves. He intended that men should participate in the self-offering and appropriate the power of his surrendered life. His redemptive service is not intended to be a work wrought apart from men; it is rather a work into which they are permitted to enter in such a way that what He does on their behalf becomes a very vital factor in their approach to God.

How empty and frivolous the Death of Christ would be unless human nature in some way was involved in sin. If we were sitting on a pier on a bright summer day, fishing contentedly, and suddenly saw another man jump off the pier in front of us into the river and, as he went down the third time, we heard him say: "Greater love than this no man hath, than he lay down his life for

A BRIEF LIFE OF CHRIST

his friend", we would have found the whole proceeding quite unintelligible.

If, however, we had fallen into the waters and were drowning, and the man came in and offered his life to save us, then there would be meaning to his Death. If human nature had not fallen into sin, the Death of Christ would be meaningless. But if He had come as the Son of God to ransom us from sin in obedience to the Father's Will and restore us to a heritage which was lost, then the Cross becomes our glory.

If we were the only persons in the world who had eyes to see, would we not be staffs to the blind; if we were the only persons in the world who were healthy, would we not minister to the sick? If we seek to identify ourselves with the physical sufferings of others because we love them, why should we not be one with those who are cast down with moral suffering? If the more healthy we are, the better we serve the sick, then the more innocent we are, the more we should take on their guilt. Eventually, this would reach a point where we would sacrifice ourselves for the other's guilt. A mother loves her child! If it were possible, she would willingly take upon herself all the pains of the child. The father will take on the debts of his son, and a lover, if possible, would take on the woes of his beloved.

Picture a chalice, which only a priest may touch, stolen from the altar. It is made into a beer mug and delivered over to profane uses. Later on, the chalice is retrieved, but before it can be restored to the altar, it must be put into the flames, the dross burned away. Then it must be beaten and hammered and refash-

Public Life and Passion

ioned again from the old creature of the beer mug, into the new creature of the chalice. Only then is it fit for blessing and ready for restoration to the altar of sacrifice.

Our human nature, which once was in possession of God's grace, and which once bore resemblance to the Divine Nature, through a free act of ours lost its dignity and became delivered over to profane and unholy purposes of sin. Our Blessed Lord came to this earth and took a human nature like ours in all things except sin. He made it stand for us as the head of the new humanity, as if He Himself were guilty for all the sins of the world. Then He takes this human nature of ours, and plunges it into the fire of Calvary to have all the dross of evil and sin burned and purged away. After being beaten and hammered and put into a grave, He finally rises from the dead as the Head of the new humanity—the Pattern Man we are destined to be if we receive His Spirit.

The whole problem of Christianity, then, is how to become incorporated again to this new humanity in Christ, Who is the Son of God. That happens, as He said, through the sending of His Spirit so that He will not be an example to be copied, but a life to be lived.

Death and Resurrection

SOME things in life are too beautiful to be forgotten, and there can also be something in death that is too beautiful to be forgotten. That is why we have a Memorial Day—to recall the sacrifices of our youth for the preservation of freedom. Freedom is not an heirloom, but a life. Once received, it does not continue to exist without effort. As life must be nourished, defended and preserved, so freedom must be repurchased in each generation. What Washington won, had to be rewon by Lincoln, then won again in World Wars I and II.

All the blood that crimsoned Valley Forge and Bunker Hill and Gettysburg, that reddened the soil of France, the Pacific Islands and Korea, cries out like Abel's blood for remembrance. Our hearts, knowing that we live because they died, answer their mute pleas by instituting a Memorial Day to recall in prayer and reverence, the sublime truth that "greater love than this no man hath, that he lay down his life for his friends."

These youths, however, were not born to die. Soldiering was an interruption to their summons to live; neither they nor their parents willed that their ship of life should be sunk so soon after launching into the sea of life. In this, all men differ from Our Blessed Lord, Who came into this world to die. Even at His Birth, His Mother was reminded that He came to *die,* as the Wise Men brought myrrh for His burial. Never before,

Death and Resurrection

did any mother see Death wrap its arms so quickly about a newborn Babe. Never before did the shadow of the Cross fall so quickly on a crib.

When He was still only an infant, the old man Simeon looked into the face of Him and said that He was destined to be a "sign to be contradicted"—a signal that would call out the opposition of the deliberately imperfect. The Mother, on hearing that word "contradicted", could almost see Simeon's arms fade and the arms of the Cross take their place to wrap Her Son in death. Before two years of His Life had been lived, King Herod sent out horsemen to decapitate Him.

Since, then, Our Divine Lord came to die, it was fitting that there be a Memorial of His death. If we keep a memorial of soldiers who died that we might be free from political oppression, then should not the Divine Soldier have a memorial for preserving us from the spiritual tyranny of sin? Since He is God, as well as man, and since He never spoke of His Death without speaking of His Resurrection, should He not Himself institute the precise memorial of His own death and not leave it to the chance recollection of men? And that is precisely what He did the night of the Last Supper. But His Memorial was instituted—and this is important—not because He would die like a soldier and be buried, but because He would live again after the Resurrection.

In His last hours with His Apostles, He instituted not a Memorial Day, but a Memorial Action. Seated at a Passover meal which commemorated the liberation of His people from the slavery of Egypt, He prepared

A BRIEF LIFE OF CHRIST

to fulfill it by celebrating the liberation of souls from the slavery of Satan! As the paschal lambs were being sacrificed to celebrate the deliverance from political slavery, He, the true Paschal Lamb, prepared to offer Himself to save souls from spiritual slavery. His act would be the New Testament; like the Old, it would be sealed with blood—not the blood of sheep, but the blood of Himself, the Immaculate Lamb.

At the Last Supper, Christ's eyes kindled and His whole bearing took on a majesty greater than when He spoke to Moses and Elias in the clouds. Taking in His hands a piece of unleavened bread, He lifted His eyes to Heaven, gave thanks, and over it said: "Take, eat, this is My Body Which shall be delivered for you." Then, taking the cup of wine, by another act of omnipotence, He breathed over it saying: "Drink, all of you, of this; for This is My Blood of the New Testament, Which shall be shed for many unto the remission of sins."

Note the words: "My Body Which shall be delivered for you; My Blood of the New Testament Which shall be shed." He was looking forward to the morrow, Good Friday, when He would die on the Cross—the one supreme reason for His coming to earth. It was a new Covenant, a new Testament. There had been one Covenant with Noah on leaving the ark, another Covenant with Abraham on leaving Haran, another with Moses on leading the people from Egypt. All led to this new Covenant between God and man. On God's side, it pledged remission of sins through His Death; on man's side, faith and sacrifice.

But how, it may be asked, does the changing of the

Death and Resurrection

Bread into His Body and the changing of the wine into His Blood, foreshadow His sacrificial Death on the Cross on the morrow? Our Lord did not consecrate the bread and wine together, but separately. This symbolic action represents the way He would be sacrificed on the Cross, namely, by the violent separation of His Blood from His Body. His Passion and His Sacrifice were beginning; on the morrow on the Cross He would be upright as a Priest, and prostrate as a Victim offering Himself for the sins of the world.

But because Our Lord's Memorial was not instituted by us, but by Him, and because He could not be conquered by death, which is a penalty for sin, but would rise again in the newness of life, He willed that as He now looked forward to His Redemptive Death on the Cross, so all the Christian ages until the consummation of the world should look back to it, the Crucifixion. In order that they would not re-enact the Memorial out of whim or fancy, He gave the command: "Do this for a commemoration of Me." That is, "Announce My redemptive Death until I come again! I will be the same Priest and Victim on both My Cross and your commemoration of My Death. But as I look forward to the Cross, you will look back to it. As this My Last Supper looks in prospect to Myself as the Victim to be immolated on Calvary, so in your commemoration you will look back to the immolation that has already taken place."

During His mortal life, Our Lord chose many varied and picturesque pulpits from which to deliver His sermons, the Words of Eternal Life. Sometimes His pulpit was Peter's bark pushed out into the sea; at other times, it was the crowded streets of Jericho, the golden gate of the Temple, Jacob's well. It seemed as if almost any pulpit pleased Him, until the day came for Him to deliver His farewell address. Then He demanded a pulpit which, like the words He was uttering, would be remembered down through the arches of the years. On Good Friday morning, as He stood on the sunlit portico of Pontius Pilate, He may have thought of making that the pulpit of His last address. There was a vast sea of faces before Him and hearts hungering for the Bread of Eternal Life—an audience like unto which anyone would have loved to open his heart.

But no, He waited a few hours for another pulpit to be given Him at the foot of the steps of Pilate's palace. That pulpit He put upon His shoulders and carried to Golgotha. That pulpit was—the Cross. Once on those heights He offered Himself to His executioners.

Hands of the Carpenter hardened by toil; hands from which the world's graces flow; feet of the Miracle Worker Who went about doing good—these now had rough nails applied to them. The first knock of the hammer was heard in silence; blow followed blow and was faintly re-echoed over the city walls beneath. Mary and John held their ears. The sound was unendurable; each echo sounded as another stroke. The cross was lifted slowly off the ground, staggered for a moment in mid-air, and then, with a thud that seemed to shake even hell itself, it sank into the pit prepared for it.

Our Lord had mounted His pulpit for the last time— and what a majestic pulpit it was! In itself the Cross

Death and Resurrection

was a sermon. How much more eloquently it spoke now when adorned with the Word of Eternal Life!

Like all who mount their pulpits, He o'erlooked His audience. Far off in the distance, across the Valley of Jehosaphat, He could see the gilded roof of the Temple reflecting its rays against the sun, which was soon to hide its face in shame. Here and there on Temple walls He caught glimpses of figures straining their eyes to catch the last view of Him whom the darkness knew not.

Nearer the pulpit, but off at the border of the crowd, stood some of His own timid disciples ready to flee in case of danger. Greeks and Romans were there, too, as well as Scribes and Pharisees from Jerusalem. There were those in the crowd asking Him to come down and prove His Divinity. There were the Deity-blind, mocking and spitting at Him. There were some who had followed Him for an hour, taunting Him that others He saved but Himself He could not save. There were Roman soldiers throwing dice for the garments of a God. And there at the foot of the cross stood that wounded flower, that broken thing, Magdalen, forgiven because she loved much. And there, with a face like a cast moulded out of love, was John. And there, God pity her, was His own Mother. Mary, Magdalen and John. Innocence, penitence and sacerdotal love — the three types of souls forever to be found beneath the Cross of Christ.

All was silence now. The Scribes and Pharisees had ceased their raillery, the Roman soldiers had put away their dice. The sky darkened and man grew fearful, awaiting the farewell address of the Son of God. He began to speak, and like all men who die, He thought of those whom He loved most. His first word was a word about His enemies: "Father forgive them, for they know not what they do." His second was about sinners as He spoke to a thief: "This day thou shalt be with Me in Paradise!" His third word was to His Mother and John. It was the new Annunciation: "Woman, behold thy son."

For Three Hours He suffered. Then there was a rupture of a Heart through the rapture of Love and He gave up His Life of His own Will. The Roman Centurion whose business it was to see that the crucified was dead, stayed at his post to the very end. Taking a spear, He pierced the Heart of the Christ. Blood and water poured out; water, the symbol of regeneration; and blood, the price of redemption.

Later Joseph of Arimathea went to beg Pilate for the body of Jesus, but Pilate would not release it until he had conducted his own investigation. He, therefore, called in the Centurion and inquired of him if He was really dead. Joseph showed no solicitude for the bodies of the two thieves. But he had a personal reverence for Jesus—he had refused in a council meeting earlier to consent to His death.

Nicodemus, who once came at night to consult Jesus, and other helpers wrapped Jesus according to custom in a sheet eight feet long and embalmed Him with spices. The Body was laid in the tomb, a great stone was rolled before the door of the sepulcher, and an official guard was set. It was the only time in history

Death and Resurrection

that a guard was set to prevent a man rising from the tomb.

In the dim dawn of the following Sunday, several women approached the tomb. The fact that they brought spices showed that they did not expect a Resurrection. It seems strange that they should have doubted, after the many references of Our Lord to His Death and His Resurrection. But whenever he predicted His Passion and Resurrection, even His disciples apparently paid more attention to His prediction of His Death than His Resurrection. It never occurred to them that His Resurrection was possible. When the stone was rolled to the door of the sepulcher, not only Christ was buried, but also all their hopes. The women thought only to anoint the body of the dead Christ, an act born of despairing and yet unbelieving love.

Two of the women at least had witnessed the burial, and their great concern was a practical one:

> Who is to roll the stone away for us
> From the door of the tomb?

It was the cry of a heart of little faith. Strong men had closed the entrance to the tomb by placing the huge stone against it; the women's worry was how to remove the barrier in order that they might carry out their errand of mercy. The men would not come to the tomb until they were summoned—so little did they believe. And the women came only because, in their grief, they sought consolation in embalming the dead.

When they came near, they saw that the stone, great

as it was, had been rolled away. They did not immediately jump to the conclusion that His Body had risen—they concluded someone had removed the Body. But then an angel whose countenance was as lightning and whose raiment was as snow said to them:

> No need to be dismayed;
> You have come to look for Jesus of Nazareth,
> Who was crucified; He has risen again,
> He is not here. Here is the place where they laid
>   Him.
> Go and tell Peter and the rest of His Disciples
> That He is going before you into Galilee.
> There you shall have sight of Him as He promised
>   you.

To an angel, the Resurrection would not be a mystery, but His Death would be. For us, the Death is not a mystery, but His Resurrection is. The angel was one keeper more than the enemies had placed about the Saviour's grave, one soldier more than Pilate had appointed.

The angel's message was the first Gospel preached after the Resurrection, and it went back again to Our Lord's Passion. When the angel spoke of Him as "Jesus of Nazareth Who was crucified", the words told: the name of His humanity, the humility of His dwelling place, and the ignominy of His Death. All three—lowliness, ignominy and shame—were brought in comparison to His arising from the dead. Bethlehem and Nazareth and Jerusalem were all made the identifying marks of His Resurrection.

Death and Resurrection

The angel's words: "Here is the place where they laid Him", confirmed the reality of His Death and the fulfillment of the ancient prophecies. We wander through a graveyard and look at tombstones almost all of which are headed with the inscription: *Hic Jacet* or "Here lies". Then follows the name of the dead, and perhaps some praise of the one departed. But here in contrast, the angel does not write, but speaks a different epitaph: "He is not here." The angel calls on the women to behold the place where their Lord's Body has laid, as though its mere desertion were evidence enough of the fact of the Resurrection. They are directed immediately to hasten and give intelligence of the Resurrection. It was to a virgin woman that the birth of the Son of God was announced. It is to a fallen woman that His Resurrection is announced.

Those who saw the empty grave were bidden to go to Peter who had tempted Our Blessed Lord once from the Cross and three times denied Him. Sin and denial cannot choke Divine Love. Paradoxical it is that the more we sin the less can we believe in His Love, and yet the more we sin and repent, the more we wonder at the marvels of His Love. It is to the lost sheep panting in the wilderness that He comes; it is the publicans and the harlots, the denying Peters and the persecuting Pauls to whom the most persuasive entreaties of love are sent. To the man who was named a Rock and who would have tempted Him from a Cross, the risen Saviour now sends through the women the message: "Go tell Peter."

Nothing is less factual than to say the pious women were expecting Christ to rise from the dead. This was, in fact, something they never expected. The other women may have rushed back to their homes, but Magdalene raced impetuously to Peter and to John, not to announce the Resurrection, but to say: "They have carried the Lord away from the tomb and we cannot tell where they have taken Him." Just a week before, she had heard her Master say that He was the Resurrection and the Life, and now instead of believing in the Resurrection, she thought that someone had stolen away the body.

Despite the multiple predictions of His Resurrection and the comparing of Himself to Jonas, still His own disciples and followers did not believe. When finally Mary Magdalene and Joanna and Mary, the mother of James, told the Apostles of His Resurrection, they refused to believe. "To their minds, the story seemed madness and they could not believe it."

Added to the original incredulity of the women was now the incredulity of the Apostles. Their answer practically was: "You know how women are, always imagining things." In vain do we think that people before the advent of scientific psychology were not afraid of their own minds playing tricks upon them. We boast of our own incredulity in the face of the extraordinary, but our scepticism is as nothing compared to the scepticism which immediately greeted the first news of the Resurrection. What modern sceptics say about the Resurrection story, the disciples themselves were the first to say. As the original agnostics of Christianity, with one assent they dismissed the whole story as a delusion. Something very extraordinary had to happen, some

Death and Resurrection

concrete evidence had to be presented to all of these doubters, before they would overcome their reluctance to believe. Their scepticism was even more difficult than modern scepticism to overcome. Theirs started from a hope that was disappointed on Calvary; that was far more difficult to heal than modern scepticism, which is without hope. Nothing is further from the truth than to say that the followers of Our Lord were expecting the Resurrection and therefore were ready to believe it or to console themselves for a loss that seemed irreparable. H.G. Wells wrote nothing about the Resurrection that the Apostles had not already had in their own minds.

After the Resurrection, Our Lord made many appearances; for example, to the disciples on the road to Emmaus, to the Apostles excluding Thomas, to multitudes, to small groups of Apostles, to Peter and John on the lake. Then after 40 days, He took leave of them to ascend, as He told Magdalen, back again to His Father. It took a long time to convince them, and the full meaning did not dawn in their souls until Pentecost. Then they were all ready to have their throats cut for their belief.

Less than seven weeks before, He had made His triumphal entry into Jerusalem; He had also suffered His ignominious death in Jerusalem, and now within view of it He would ascend back again to His Father. While in the city He opened their understanding, gave them the light beyond the light of reason. However excellent natural and external means may be, they still are insufficient; fullness of faith only God can give. Once that new understanding or new light comes, then everything appears differently than it was before. The difference is the same as two men walking into a room, one man being blind and the other man having eyes to see. Both have some approximation of the contents of the room, but only the man with eyes understands clearly each object and the relation of one to another. So when He opened their understanding, the words *Christ* and *sin* and *suffering* all had different sounds in their ears, and a different meaning in their hearts. He might have illumined their minds without any appeal to reason or history, but the practical method that He chose was the historical one. He told them all the things that had been written in the law of Moses and the Prophets and the Psalms, concerning Him, in order that they might understand the Scriptures. That these men about Him should have, in a single second, understood the full scope of history is as great a miracle as any of His healings.

Then He came back to the basic idea of His Life, namely, that He came on this earth not to live, but to suffer and die, to redeem and to be glorified. Bringing into one focal point all He had told them about the Scriptures, He said:

> So it was written and so it was fitting
> That Christ should suffer, and should rise again
> From the dead on the third day; and that repentance
> And remission of sins should be preached in
> His name to all nations, beginning at Jerusalem.
> Of this you are the witnesses.

Death and Resurrection

He said God's redemptive purpose was being revealed in the Prophets, and this redemption was to be effective by the death of the God Who became man. Once more there is a total absence of the fact that He was to leave a code or a set of rules. He emphasized the fact that His death made possible the preaching of repentance and the remission of sins to all nations and to all peoples. He said that it behooved Him to suffer. This indeed was true, because when anyone preaches absolute and Divine Truth to a world that believes in pragmatism, He will be crucified. The only way that He could show the evil of sin, was by revealing what sin could do to goodness, namely, pinion Him to a tree. If sin is a debt, that debt can be paid only by someone Who gave His life in ransom. It is very likely that He retold for them the story of God telling Abraham to sacrifice his son Isaac as a burnt offering. From the moment of that command, Isaac was a dead man, but on the third day he was released from his death sentence. He probably told them the Psalms wherein it was said of Him:

Thou shalt not leave my soul in hell,
Nor suffer Thy own Holy One to see corruption.

His death alone would have had no efficacy for the removal of human guilt, if He had not broken the bonds of the grave. Arising from the dead, He showed that the Redemption price paid on Calvary was sufficient, and that it was accepted by His Heavenly Father.

Now He commissioned them as His witnesses to bring repentance to all nations. When Our Blessed

Lord began His public life one of His first words was "repent". It was also the subject of His departing breath. Repentance and the remission of sins are twins; almost Siamese twins, for they cannot be separated. Repentance sees the rubbish in the temple of the body, but remission of sins drives out those buyers and sellers and makes it truly a house of prayer.

This preaching of the remission of sins was to begin at Jerusalem where He was crucified, in order that not even the place which took His life is to be exempted from His forgiveness. Those who have had great privileges and who have apparently rejected them, are not to be considered beyond the hope of forgiveness. The conversion of the world starts at home, but it only starts there. Then the Saviour said:

> And behold, I am sending down upon you
> The Gift which was promised by My Father;
> You must wait in the city until you are
> Clothed with power from on high.

Christ told the Apostles to tarry in Jerusalem until He sent His Spirit. If He had remained on earth, they could have heard His voice, touched His hand, seen His radiant face, but if He ascended to His Father and sent His Spirit, then He would be a veritable life to be lived. This Spirit, He said, would recall to their minds all things He had told them. The Spirit would not be a code of morality written either on tablets of their minds or on tablets of stone, but would enter into their will and motivate their actions, penetrate the intellect

Death and Resurrection

to see truths beyond the power of reason, encourage them to love the things that He loved, and inspire them to enter into their glory as He entered into His—by dying to atone for the evil of the world.

The Spirit would not be long in coming—only 10 days hence. The Apostles were to keep their eyes in expectation upon the horizon and their hand upon the door; God in His own pleasure would endow them from a power on high. This power would not only awaken the soul of man from the deadly sleep of sin, but it would also be the comforter of the soul and above all, the source of their sanctification.

After giving them the promise of the Spirit, Our Blessed Lord led His disciples out as far as Bethany and lifted up His hands and blessed them.

> And even as He blessed them He parted from them,
> And was carried up into heaven.

He had promised His disciples that they would follow Him and be with Him, and that He would go to Heaven to prepare a place for them. Great is the contrast between the unimaginable grandeur of the Ascension, and the sober words with which the record is set down. The night of the Last Supper He told His Apostles that He was soon to enter into the glory with His Father that He had before the foundations of the world were laid. He also told Pilate that He would see the Son of Man coming on the right hand of His power to judge the living and the dead. Now, He became the forerunner of Humanity in heaven.

A BRIEF LIFE OF CHRIST

The Apostles must have noticed, as He blessed them upon leaving, the great scars of Redemption on His hands. Peter in particular must have recalled that they were the same hands that saved Him from the Galilean waves; Thomas must have lamented that it was the hand that He was bidden to touch to be cured of His doubt; all of the Apostles must have remembered that He showed them those same sacred hands to remind them that this was the mission for which He came to earth. But now that they were believing, the marks at this time were less the record of a Crucifixion than the record of a love of One Who lay down His life for His sheep.

The Ascension was necessary to equip His Apostolic Body for their universal mission. By withdrawing His bodily presence to that unseen region, which bears no special relation to any nation or people, He proclaims in the Ascension the common destiny of all the adopted sons of God. Even the best of men would not feel at home in Heaven with all of its splendor unless they would find there One Who was their brother in the Fatherhood of God. Joseph's brethren would have felt ill at ease in one of the most regal courts of the world, if their brother were not already there upon the throne. When He ascended into Heaven, He took with Himself His human nature which is like our own in all things, save sin. When He took upon Himself this human nature from His Mother Mary, He made it possible for Himself to suffer. She gave Him a body on which might be visited all the effects of sin, though He Himself was sinless. His birth and His life, therefore,

Death and Resurrection

made Him a victim for sacrifice and identified Him with the human race. The Ascension was necessary in order to bring Him into a state of perfect union with the Father, and in order to send the Spirit that we might be other Christs.

His continued life in Heaven, with His Glorified Humanity, is accepted by the Father on His Mercy Seat as our Intercessor. Once He offered Himself for us, the just for the unjust, whenever we identify ourselves with Him as victim, we behold in Him the expiation of our sins, and also our admission into the presence of the Father. All humanity is potentially with Him in Heaven after His Ascension, inasmuch as he is the new Adam or the Son of Man; the *actualization* of each human being as His brother or as an adopted son of the Heavenly Father, depends upon man's response to the Spirit. In Heaven, He lives to make intercession for us. In Him, all humanity will stand in such unity of love to the Father, that the Father will love all men as His sons; the Father will pour out upon all who will believe in Him the same blessings that he once poured out upon Him as the Head of humanity.

During His earthly life, He solicited us to avail ourselves of Redemption by seeing what sin cost. The evil of sin is the Crucifixion of the God-man. The worst thing that sin can do is not to bomb cities or kill children, but to crucify Goodness. No man is ever conscious of sin, when he thinks of it as merely breaking a law. He never sees the full intensity of sin until be realizes what he does to a person. Many an alcoholic does not know the evil of his sin until, driving while drunk, he kills a child. So when we look not to a broken law, but at the broken Person of Christ on the Cross, we begin to see the full gravity of sin. We see it in the nails and in the crown of thorns, but we also see the love of God Who goes on loving us despite our sins.

On the Cross, Our Lord poured out His Life's Blood, not because bloodshed pleased His Father, but because the sinner deserved to die, and Christ, willing to be one with sinners, chose to bear pain as they should have borne it. He bore all of the iniquity of evil because He deigned to come into the world disorganized by evil.

If we would see the world at its worst, look at the Cross on Good Friday! The world will never do anything quite as evil as it did that day! There was darkness over the earth then, the sun refusing to shed its light on the crime that would extinguish the Light of the World! There is darkness over the world today as there was then, and for the same reason, because Christ is re-crucified in those who believe and confess His Name. Giant curtains are pulled over the Light of the World: Iron Curtains, Bamboo Curtains, and Plush Curtains. Iron curtains are pulled down in Eastern Europe where in Stygian night, hammers and sickles beat and cut. But a day will come when He will lay hold of that hammer, hold it aloft in His Resurrected, Scarred Hand, and make it look like a Cross, and the sickle will appear as the moon under Our Lady's Feet. Bamboo curtains have been pulled over China, where in the night, missionaries are ridiculed before other Pilates, slapped before other Caaphases, and beaten in other Praetoria. But as hundreds of thousands of Chinese suffer and die in His Name, and in union with His Cross, they prepare a day when the sun will rise again in the East—a sun that will be the Light of the World! Plush curtains too, of American and Western civilization have been pulled over Christ, until we work in the murky mist of self-sufficiency, of plenty, of confused idealism and deflated morality.

What do we see written across the map of the world but blood! Soldiers' blood poured out on Korean rocks; martyrs' blood crimsoning Chinese earth; Jewish blood but recently dried from Nazi persecutions in Buchenwalds and now dampened again by Christian blood in the Communist persecution; pagan blood poured charitably into blood banks to aid soldiers wounded in the bloody business of war. God never intended us to live in a world of constant hemorrhage.

We know the answer! Neither animal blood in sacrifice, nor human blood were meant to cataract and cascade over this globe. His Blood alone paid the debt of our sins! It is because we invoke not the Blood of Christ that we shed one another's blood in war. When we see His Death as Redemption, believe in Him as the Son of God Who made amends for our sins, then will this crimson scourge cease!

www.ingramcontent.com/pod-product-compliance
Lightning Source LLC
Chambersburg PA
CBHW030726150426
42813CB00051B/242